FATE Presents

MYSTERIES OF THE AFTERLIFE

FATE Presents
MYSTERIES OF THE AFTERLIFE

Compiled & Edited by
Rosemary Ellen Guiley

Visionary Living Publishing/Visionary Living, Inc.
New Milford, Connecticut

Fate Presents
Mysteries of the Afterlife

Compiled and edited by Rosemary Ellen Guiley

Copyright Visionary Living, Inc. 2018

All rights reserved.
No part of this book may be used or reproduced
without permission from the publisher.

Cover by April Slaughter
Interior and back jacket design by Leslie McAllister

ISBN: 978-1-942157-37-3 (pbk)
ISBN: 978-1-942157-38-0 (ebook)

Visionary Living Publishing/Visionary Living, Inc.
New Milford, Connecticut
www.visionarylivingpublishing.com

Table of Contents

Introduction ix

Near-Death Experiences
On the Psychic Frontier: Near-Death Experiences · *D. Scott Rogo*   3
A New Look at the Near-Death Phenomenon · *PMH Atwater*   11
Near Death and Out of the Body · *Christopher Bloom*   21
Return from Death · *Ronald L. Voreis*   31
Men Who Came Back from the Dead · *Edmund P. Gibson*   37
My Journey into Light · *Douglas DeLong*   41
A Closer Look at Betty Eadie's Near-Death Experience · *Scott S. Smith*   47
Near-Death Experiences of Children · *PMH Atwater*   55
Visionary Business · *Frank Spaeth*   65
An Unconventional Near-Death Experience · *Bruce Pont*   71
The Girl Who Died ... Again · *Michael T. Shoemaker*   77
Beyond the Etheric Veil · *Ernest Groth*   79

Visionary Experiences and Transformation
Spiritual, Mystical and Extraordinary Experiences: Life-Changing Transformations · *Bob Davis, PhD*   83
Near-Death Visions of the Future · *Kenneth Ring, PhD*   93
In the Shadow of Death · *PMH Atwater*   103
Flight to the Afterlife · *Freda Quenneville*   115
The Portal at Ground Zero · *Joyce Keller*   119

Dying, Death and Survival
Life After Death: Historical and New Evidence · *Rodger I. Anderson*   129
An Interview with Dr. Elisabeth Kübler-Ross · *James Crenshaw*   149
The Psychic World of Dying Children · *D. Scott Rogo*   161
Let My Brother Go · *Patti Paster*   171
Suffering During the Dying Process Has a Purpose · *Rebecca Conroy-Costello*   175

Why the Christian Church Must Study Survival ·
Reverend Robert E. Allen   179
What It Is Like to Die · *Jerry Stanley*   187

Heaven and Hell

Visions of the Next World · *Paula Giovetti*   197
Swedenborg: The Man Who Talked with Angels · *Jerome Kearful*   209
Is There A Hell? · *D. Scott Rogo*   219
The Less Than Positive Near-Death Experience ·
Barbara R. Rommer, MD   227
Judgment Day! · *Michael Newton*   235

About FATE   241
About Rosemary Ellen Guiley   243

Introduction

Human beings have known since ancient times that another world awaits us after death, where the soul carries on. We see the evidence of this knowledge in the ways we have treated and buried the dead: they are prepared for a journey and given sacred passage to the afterlife. We preserve our links to them with memorials and remembrances, ancestral altars and ceremonies.

Our visions, dreams and experiences of life after death have been recorded through the ages. Remarkable similarities from era to era, culture to culture, reveal a consistent picture of what happens to us after we die. Death is not the end, but a transition. Research offers compelling data, but sometimes the best reassurance comes from the personal experiences of those who have looked across the threshold to the world beyond, and have returned to the world of the living to talk about it.

Since its beginnings in 1948, FATE magazine has published in every issue – more than 700 to date – testimonies and articles about death, dying, the afterlife, near-death experiences (NDEs), reunions with the dead, and related topics. Articles have been contributed by leading scientists and researchers in the field, and by experiencers whose lives were transformed by an NDE or reunion with a departed loved one.

Now this special anthology of the best of FATE, plus new articles, makes a wealth of information on the afterlife available.

Twenty-nine articles are arranged in four sections:

Near-Death Experiences showcases dramatic personal accounts of trips to the edge of the afterlife, and what people learned from their experiences. For most, they lose their doubt and uncertainty about survival, as well as fear of death. This section also includes research findings and conclusions from leading experts in the field. PMH Atwater and D. Scott Rogo are among the authors. Featured in the articles are NDE researchers such as Kenneth Ring, Michael Sabom, Bruce Greyson and Raymond Moody.

Visionary Experiences and Transformations starts with an exceptional article by Bob Davis on scientific research on the types and characteristics of life-changing events such as NDEs. In addition, Kenneth Ring, one of the pioneers in NDE research, describes the visions of the future had by NDErs, and psychic Joyce Keller gives a moving account of helping souls who perished in the 9/11 World Trade Center disaster.

Dying, Death and Survival features among its articles the ground-breaking research of Elizabeth Kübler-Ross, accounts of the experiences of children, and an excellent article on why the Christian Church should study survival – not all the answers are in the Bible.

Heaven and Hell examines positive and negative NDEs and states in the afterlife. Is there a "final judgment" or is the afterlife a place of redemption? Many NDEs contradict final judgment and consignment for eternity to a heaven or a hell. Rather, the afterlife is a place where souls continue to grow.

The articles have been published throughout the history of FATE to present times, and the publication dates are given at the ends.

From start to finish, *Mysteries of the Afterlife* provides provocative reading. If you are searching for answers, you will find information from different perspectives. If you are grieving, you will find comfort.

I also recommend *Contact with the Dead*, a sister volume of FATE articles, which features the many ways we have spontaneous contact with the dead or can initiate it.

– Rosemary Ellen Guiley,
Executive Editor, FATE

NEAR-DEATH EXPERIENCES

ON THE PSYCHIC FRONTIER: NEAR-DEATH EXPERIENCES
D. Scott Rogo

When public and scientific interest in the near-death experience (NDE) surged in the 1970s, there were two rival theories for such encounters. One group of researchers felt that the experience was real. Perhaps something really did "separate" from the brain and fly to the Great Beyond. Other researchers decried this simplistic and basically metaphysical model, claiming that the experience was merely hallucinatory.

Neither side won this scientific battle. Those researchers taking a literalist view of the NDE couldn't explain the fact that cultural beliefs contaminate the experience. The debunkers and skeptics, on the other hand, couldn't cope with Dr. Michael Sabom's evidence (presented in *Recollections of Death*) that people undergoing NDEs sometimes "watch" and correctly report on their surgical operations.

This long-standing stalemate between the believers and the skeptics has entered into its second chapter. Some researchers interested in the NDE have begun focusing on the neurology and neurophysiology of the experience.

If the experience is real, what changes in the brain result from leaving the body? If the experience is a complex hallucination, where in the brain is it encoded?

The possibility that the NDE represents a phenomenon linked specifically to events within the brain was originally suggested in the 1970s. The first researchers to suggest this model were the Czech-born psychiatrist Dr. Stanislav Grof and his (then) wife, the internationally known anthropologist Dr. Joan Halifax. They tackled the puzzle of the NDE in 1977, two years after the original publication of Dr. Raymond Moody's pioneering *Life After Life*.

In their book *The Human Encounter with Death*, Drs. Grof and Halifax suggested that NDEs were coded into the brain and "emerged" when the organ underwent life-threatening stress. The two researchers never posited where in the brain such a complex phenomenon was coded, nor by what neurobiological process it emerged.

The concept of the "encoded experience" did, however, explain the inner consistency to which NDEs conform. That the NDE could be a purely neurophysiological phenomenon was reinforced in 1980 by UCLA psychopharmacologist Dr. Ronald Siegel who showed that NDEs and hallucinations produced by psychoactive chemicals (such as LSD) share considerable ground. Dr. Siegel published his observations in a lengthy paper in the *American Psychologist*. The article received considerable play in the popular press – much to the consternation of its writer, who received death threats, dung and Bibles filled with bullets from people who didn't like his views!

Again, the specific neurological mechanism by which these episodes emerge was left undescribed.

The basic ingredients for a comprehensive neurophysiological explanation of the NDE dates only from 1982, when Dr. Daniel Carr – a Boston physician – drew upon the recent discovery of natural opiates in the brain in building his theory. (For some background into the discovery of these chemicals, called endorphins and enkephalins, see Jeff Goldberg's *Anatomy of a Scientific Discovery*, published in 1988.) These peptides have the (purported) power to induce pleasure, elevate mood and produce anesthesia in people. Dr. Carr suggested that these

"Ascent of the Blessed" by Hieronymous Bosch, created between 1500-1504.
Credit: Wikimedia Commons.

chemicals were the biological triggers for the NDE and could explain the positive emotions reported by NDE survivors.

How do NDEs happen?

Dr. Carr posited that endorphins released near death stimulate the hippocampus, a small organ within the brain that constitutes part of the limbic system. The limbic system is a group of organs in the "older" section of the brain, from the standpoint of evolution, and takes part in regulating our primitive emotions. The limbic system is in turn buried deep within the brain's temporal lobes, which produce sensory hallucinations when stimulated.

Dr. Carr suggested that NDEs are deeply moving hallucinations caused by a cascade effect: Chemical stimulation within the hippocampus spreads to the limbic system, which spreads to the temporal lobe where it causes vivid hallucinations. The Boston physician supported his theory by referring to considerable biochemical findings on the endorphins and other neurohormones. The final version of his conceptual model was published in the June 1982 issue of *Anabiosis: The Journal for Near-Death Studies, Volume 2, Number 1*.

While his biochemical model was ingenious, there was a critical flaw in Dr. Carr's thinking. Endorphins function in the brain similar to narcotics such as morphine, since they bind to the same neural receptors. We should expect considerable common ground between morphine hallucinations and the characteristics of the classical NDE. That's where Dr. Carr's theory falls apart, for morphine hallucinations resemble vivid nightmares completely unlike the NDE.

While the release of endorphins has been rejected by NDE researchers as the primary source of the NDE, some elements from Carr's original model have shown up in second generation neurophysiological theories for the NDE. Could the experience, for example, be "located" within the temporal lobes? (These lobes fold under the brain's frontal cortex, which constitutes the seat of mankind's executive and planning functions.) The possible role the temporal lobes play in the NDE is the controversy which I'd like to discuss.

Role of temporal lobes

The first comprehensive temporal lobe model for the NDE was presented in the Summer 1989 issue of the *Journal of Near-Death Studies* by Dr. Juan C. Saavedra-Aguilar and Dr. Juan S. Gomez-Jeria of the University of Chile. Here is their theory briefly summarized:

The two researchers begin their paper by pointing out that seizures within the temporal lobes can cause both sensory and motor disturbances, including:

1) strange physical sensations within the body

2) localized tremors and even complex movements and behavior

3) rising and sinking feelings

4) visual hallucinations

5) intense emotional changes

6) flashbacks and distortions in self-perception

Within this range of temporal lobe symptoms lie the "building blocks of the NDE," suggest the Chilean researchers.

By what mechanism is the complex phenomenology of the NDE built?

The Chilean researchers tackle this issue by drawing upon the same neurological factors Carr used in 1982 – that biological stress releases endorphins into the limbic system. This phenomenon is well known to brain experts and is not mere speculation. This chemical overload hyperstimulates the limbic system/temporal lobes, suggest the South American neurologists, a situation compounded by lack of oxygen to the brain in general.

The resulting rapid firing of neurons within the temporal lobes (technically called disinhibition) would produce a range of hallucinations that the brain could "interpret" as an NDE.

The brain performs this function, they posit, by piecing together scattered phenomenology in terms of the patient's cultural expectations. In other words, the brain – trying to make sense of their hallucinations –

structures them and transfers them into a linguistic form that conforms to the subject's religio-cultural beliefs.

Mixed reactions from neurological experts

Dr. Bruce Greyson, editor of the *Journal of Near-Death Studies*, realized that the Chilean researchers' proposals were controversial. When he published their paper, he invited nine neurological experts to comment on it. The Summer 1989 issue of the *Journal* contained these critical commentaries.

Most of the paper's discussants offered their congratulations to the Chilean researchers.

Some researchers found the proposals of the Chilean researchers extremely flawed. Several criticisms of their conceptual model for the NDE were given by Dr. Glen O. Gabbard and Dr. Stuart W. Twemlow, two psychiatrists from Kansas interested in NDE research. They pointed out in their rebuttal that:

> 1) The symptomatology of temporal lobe epilepsy is so inclusive that anything, theoretically, could be linked to it.
>
> 2) The Kansas psychiatrists especially criticize their colleagues for confusing similarity with causation. Because two psychological experiences resemble each other doesn't mean they are produced by the same mechanism.
>
> 3) The model proposed by the Chilean researchers is based on chemical signals produced when the brain undergoes stress. Some people, however, experience NDE-like episodes spontaneously when they are facing neither death nor biological stress.

The debate over the neurological model proposed by Dr. Saavedra-Aguilar and Dr. Gomez-Jeria is bound to continue, but theirs is not the last word on the NDE and temporal lobe function. Hardly had the furor over their model settled than a rival neurophysiological model was presented in the subsequent issue of the *Journal of Near-Death Studies*!

NDEs and children

For some time now, Dr. Melvin Morse and his colleagues at the University of Washington have been studying NDEs reported by children. They have been impressed by the consistency of the experiences claimed by children near death. Even their drawings of their perceptions look surprisingly alike. Such findings have suggested to Dr. Morse that the NDE is probably directly encoded into the brain, not pieced together in the manner suggested by Drs. Saavedra-Aguilar and Gomez-Jeria. But where in the brain? By what neural mechanisms does it enter consciousness?

In order to explain these problems, Dr. Morse draws upon the pioneering research of the late Dr. Wilder Penfield, a Canadian neurosurgeon who experimented in the 1940s and 1950s with electrically stimulating his patients' brains while they were undergoing surgery to correct intractable epilepsy. Dr. Penfield discovered that stimulation to the cortex of the temporal lobes resulted in visual hallucinations, hearing music and eerie sensations of leaving the body. These sound suspiciously like the fundamental components of the NDE. The Canadian surgeon even mapped out where in the cortex these sensations can be evoked.

Believing that he has found the location of the NDE within the brain, Dr. Morse next proposes the precise neurochemical trigger that leads to its emergence into consciousness. The brain is partly regulated by neurotransmitters, chemicals involved with everything from mood to sleep to our perception of pain.

Serotonin is one of these primary neurotransmitters especially linked to the regulation of our sleep/wake cycles and everyday moods. Serotonin seems to be implicated in our response to threat when it is produced in high levels to relieve stress and calm our reactions. Dr. Morse and his colleagues suggest that this chemical – ubiquitous within the brain – somehow triggers the temporal lobes to "release" the NDE in the face of imminent danger or death.

The Washington physician is careful, however, to point out that his model is not reductionistic by nature. "Although much of our work is speculative," he explains, "it is well documented that neuronal connections specific for creating out-of-body states exist. Such genetically determined areas in our brains may well serve as a natural defense mechanism against stressful situations, such as childbirth or trauma, both of which have been reported to cause OBEs. However, it is just as likely that such an area represents the seat of the soul, the area of our brain that serves as a trigger point for the release of the soul at death. Such an area could serve equally well for stresses during life. This would also explain how certain religions use control of the autonomic nervous system, which is integrally enmeshed with the hippocampus and limbic structures, to produce out-of-body states and religious ecstasy."

In other words, perhaps the NDE really does – in the final run – represent the release of the soul.

D. Scott Rogo (1950-1990): FATE *columnist and prolific author and writer. This article was his last for* FATE, *published after his murder on August 18, 1990.*

FATE September 1990

A NEW LOOK AT THE NEAR-DEATH PHENOMENON
PMH Atwater

A 1992 Gallup Poll found that around 1.3 million adults claimed to have had at least one near-death experience. That's roughly one-third of those who face death in a hospital or clinical setting at any time. For children the figure is 75 per cent, as established by Melvin Morse, MD. Morse, Kimberly Clark Sharp, MSW, and a team of associates conducted the first empirical study of children's near-death experiences.

These percentages, as large as they are, barely touch upon what is currently happening. It is time to reconsider what we think we know about the near-death phenomenon. In my book, *Beyond the Light: What Isn't Being Said About the Near-Death Experience,* the NDE is further explored. I wrote the book to explore the positive and negative aspects of the phenomenon, its aftereffects, and its implications. My research was based on original interviews conducted over more than 15 years of continuous study.

If you say the phrase "near-death experience" today, most people still connect it with Raymond Moody, Jr., MD. He coined the term in his 1975 bestseller, *Life After Life,* a work that established NDEs as a legitimate field of study. There were, however, a number of people who researched NDEs before Moody. Among them was Brad Steiger, who wrote of "pseudo death experiences" in his 1968 work, *World Beyond Death,* and again in his 1971 book, *Minds Through Space and Time.* *[Editor's note: FATE published an article on an NDE in its premier issue in 1948. See "Beyond the Etheric Veil" at the end of this section.]*

Other researchers who wrote on the subject after Moody include Maurice Rawlings, MD, with his 1978 treatise on the hellish aspects of NDEs; Kenneth Ring, PhD, and his 1980 scientific approach; and Michael B. Sabom, MD, with his 1982 clinical findings that elevated near-death research to new heights of credibility. More than 80 people are researching the near-death phenomenon in the US and dozens more in countries around the world.

For experiencers, opening up about what happened to them has been a slow and sometimes painful process, with family and friends not necessarily being supportive or encouraging. Betty J. Eadie's book, *Embraced by the Light,* has changed that. With sales in the millions, she has proved that a near-death survivor's point of view is just as important as that of a researcher. Eadie's was not the first such effort by an experiencer, but it was her book that firmly captured the public's attention.

People like me, who are both experiencers and researchers, have a special challenge to examine the near-death phenomenon through the unique lens of having been there. Our studies and investigations invariably challenge details put forth by both dispassionate researchers and impassioned experiencers. And we face the specter of bias in ways others do not.

Three near-death experiences

A miscarriage turned nightmare nearly ended my life three times in three months during early 1977 and resulted in three different near-death events. That fall I had three relapses, one of which was adrenal failure. Although I cannot prove that I was dead during any of these episodes, it is the opinion of medical specialists that I did indeed die.

I launched my study of the phenomenon the next year, after meeting Elizabeth Kübler-Ross at Chicago's O'Hare Airport and being told by her that I was a near-death survivor. Her explanation of what I had gone through helped, but not enough. My questions were too numerous.

The research I initiated quickly became an ongoing, nearly seven-days-a-week affair. Kenneth Ring, PhD, a scientific NDE researcher, invited me to write a column in *Vital Signs* magazine (then a publication of the International Association for Near-Death Studies, IANDS). I began publishing my findings, especially about the aftereffects, in 1981.

Those early observations described an apparently universal pattern of psychological aftereffects that the average experiencer goes through, as chronicled in *Coming Back to Life: The After Effects of the Near-Death Experience*. Melvin Morse, MD, has since verified my discoveries.

To date, I have spoken with or interviewed over 3,000 near-death survivors. I mention only 700, however, in *Beyond the Light,* since that number more closely addresses those I have interviewed in depth.

Caucasian Americans, Europeans and Arabs constitute nearly 80 per cent of my subjects. I did not meet any experiencers who were East Asian. Approximately 20 per cent of those I interviewed were black (15 per cent African American, five per cent divided among Kenya, Haiti and Canada).

Four types of experiences

If you keep an individual's near-death episode in context with the life he or she lived, not only do you find correlations and connections, you also find startling, repetitive patterns. Four types of NDEs emerge, and each reveals far more than you might think. All four types can occur during the same near-death episode, or they might be spread across a series of events for a particular individual. Each, though, represents a distinctive type of experience that occurs just once to a given person. Value and meaning depend on each person involved and his or her response to what happened (including the aftereffects).

The initial near-death experience, sometimes referred to as the "non-experience," involves elements such as a loving nothingness, the living dark or a friendly voice. It is usually experienced by those who seem to need the least amount of evidence for proof of survival, or who need the least amount of shaking up in their lives.

Experiencers of this type respond afterward as if suddenly stimulated. They appear to be more alert, curious and open to new ideas than they were before. Their sensory faculties sometimes heighten; they start to think more creatively and abstractly.

I suspect brain chemistry must be affected or altered in some manner because of the way initial experiencers tend to emphasize feelings and imagery over substance. Yet these people are more than just stimulated. They seem to wake up to a deeper awareness of life's meaning.

A second type of encounter is the unpleasant and/or hell-like encounter. This type usually deals with a threatening void, stark limbo, hellish purgatory or scenes of a startling and unexpected indifference. It can even include hauntings from one's own past. It is usually experienced by those who have deeply suppressed or repressed guilts, fears and angers, or by those who expect some kind of punishment or discomfort after death.

I did not find the heavy concentration of unpleasant and/or hell-like experiences among Bible-belt Christians as some researchers claim, but I did discover that only those more influenced by fundamentalist religious beliefs ever reported hell as hot and fiery.

Whether or not an individual could cope with his or her scenario had more to do with the hellish label than with actual content. Surprisingly, just as many experiencers expressed gratitude at having undergone an episode of this type as those who were upset or frightened by it. Only adults ever reported a hell-like scenario.

The unpleasant and/or hellish version of near-death seems to be a confrontation with one's own shadow, that aspect of self either repressed or denied. Because of this, unpleasant experiences often foster opportunities for inner purification, cleaning house on levels deeper and more powerful than that of personal or religious beliefs. Since it seems to function as a mechanism the psyche uses for healing and for growth, I no longer consider the hell-like experience negative.

A third type of near-death experience is the pleasant and/or heaven-like experience. These feature scenarios of loving family reunions with those who have previously died, reassuring religious figures or light beings, validation that life counts, and affirmative and inspiring dialogue. It is usually experienced by those who most need to know how loved they are and how important life is.

Just as I no longer consider the hell-like experience negative, I no longer refer to the pleasant and/or heaven-like experience as positive.

That's because some experiencers are traumatized by it or become such messianic zealots afterward that they become more of a menace than an inspiration. Labeling an experience as heavenly addresses more how people respond to what happened than it does the content of the experience. What one experiencer calls wondrous, another often terms horrendous.

The need to feel loved

The need to feel loved and accepted, part of something grander, was the overriding link in every case of the pleasant and/or heaven-like experience. (This was true also of children, although many times this seemed more of an issue for the parents than the child.) Experiencing true love and coming to know what it is can be so fulfilling that an experiencer may feel pressured to pass the gift on. That sense of mission wraps itself around themes of accountability and moral upliftment.

Just as joy can be as instructive as pain, so too can the heavenly experience be as much a tool for healing and growth as the hellish version.

I label the last type of near-death experience transcendent. This fourth type may involve exposure to otherworldly dimensions and scenes beyond the individual's frame of reference. It sometimes includes revelations of greater truths. This experience is usually undergone by those who are ready for a mind-stretching challenge, and/or are most apt to utilize the truths that are revealed to them.

The criteria used to determine these experiences was as follows:

- Was the scenario primarily impersonal?
- Was it otherworldly enough to stretch the individual's belief systems beyond anything previously known or imagined?
- Was the experiencer radically changed afterward, almost as if he or she had become another person?
- How compelled was the individual to use his or her experience to make a significant contribution to the world? Did the individual do anything about this compulsion?

Transcendent cases are powerful in both content and consequences, but they are risky business in the way that they can affect experiencers' lives and the lives of countless others. The force of information that emerges can easily be distorted or can prove less than useful. Experiencers of this type often take on a saintly appearance afterward and usually possess great charm, charisma, and persuasive powers. Miracles are common in their presence, including healings. Because of this, it can be difficult for the average person to separate truth from personal passion when around them.

Many historical examples of transcendent cases can be found. Around 300 BC the Greek philosopher Plato wrote of Er the soldier, who revived on a funeral pyre after being dead for 10 days and then began to preach about the spiritual truths he had learned while on the other side.

In 1837, Hung Hsiu-ch'uan lay dying for 40 days when a dramatic near-death vision restored his health. Six years later, he used a Christian missionary pamphlet to validate his experience and prove that he had been chosen by God to free China of evil influences. The God Worshippers Society he established became an army used to launch a bloody civil war. Twenty million Chinese were killed. Hung changed his name to Tien Wang (The Heavenly King) and claimed the Chinese Imperial throne for himself.

People who undergo the transcendent experience are confronted by the dilemma of whether to inspire power over or power to others. Each one faces it to some degree.

Nor is there any single experiencer whose case is the most profound, or better, or more complete than the others. Any such claim is strictly media hype or the result of someone's personal opinion. Newer cases are topping older ones in profundity and dazzlement every day.

Children's encounters

Consider the cases of children. Even newborns can have a near-death experience, remember it, and, when old enough to speak, tell their parents about it. It's children who speak of an animal heaven they must pass through before they can be in the heaven where people are. Often, children encounter a sibling who died before them. Future siblings are also met. Such reports have been verified consistently.

When you consider the aftereffects, you come to realize that the near-death phenomenon reveals more about life than it does about death.

In those cases where experiencers claim to have aftereffects, 80 to 90 per cent exhibit physiological changes as well as psychological. The most frequent are:

- Looking and acting younger; being more playful
- Having skin brighten, eyes sparkle; smiling more
- Having substantially more or less energy
- Becoming sensitive to any form of light, especially sunlight
- Becoming sensitive to any form of sound and to noise levels
- Having levels of boredom decreased or increased
- Handling stress easier; healing quicker from hurts and wounds
- Brain begins to function differently

Seventy-three per cent of the people in my research base reported electrical sensitivity. Electrical sensitivity is a term near-death researchers use to refer to those people whose energy seems to affect or control electrical and/or electronic equipment, sometimes causing malfunctions, breakage, or other unusual reactions that cannot be rationally explained. I admit to being rather surprised when I sent out a questionnaire to 100 people to further explore what might be happening in this regard. Forty-six people replied.

With the questionnaire and through additional interviews, I made a link between the light experienced during a near-death scenario and the degree of sensitivity to light, sound and electrical sensitivity that an experiencer displays afterwards. Instead of amounts of exposure being the deciding factor, I found that it is the intensity of the light that makes the difference. In other words, quality of light, not quantity.

Consider the most common negative aftereffects of the near-death experience: initial confusion and disorientation; disappointment with the unresponsive or uncaring attitudes of others; depression and the inability to translate the experience into daily life; behavior that becomes threatening to others; appearing to others as arrogant and unloving; displays of a domineering know-it-all aloofness; and/or claims of divine authority for one's actions.

Compare that with the most common positive aftereffects of near-death: being unconditionally loving and generous; being unhindered, detached, childlike; having a heightened sense of the present moment; having enhanced sensitivities and a greater awareness of the needs of others, an expanded world view, and fewer worries or fears; having knowledge of one's spiritual identity and a grander purpose to life and/or willing to be accountable for one's actions.

The myth of amazing grace, created by some near-death researchers and blown out of proportion by every television talk show host in the industry, goes like this: As a compensatory gift, near-death experiencers are privileged to survive the immediacy of death and to witness, in so doing, the realms of heaven. They return utterly transformed, eschewing greed and materialism for selfless service and love for all humankind. This just is not so.

The near-death phenomenon is a complex dynamic that addresses a broad range of issues. Just for starters:

- Since infants, even newborns, can accurately remember the experience and conditions of their birth, how much more can they remember, and how far back does their memory go? How does this speak to the penchant in our country to operate on little ones without benefit of anesthesia? If they can remember a near-death experience, can they not remember that surgery?

- Since out-of-body episodes often have components in them that are later verified, some even impossibly so, what does this say about our range of faculties? Also, what does this say about the relationship between our faculties and our brain? And about our ability to be completely mobile and fully functional without a body and still be in possession of all our faculties?

- Since near-death survivors are physically changed by their experience, as well as psychologically, what does this say about the real power of subjective experiences? Does this not mean that we need to redefine subjectivity itself and its value to the continuance of a healthy life? And what about the structural changes that occur to the brain? What does this mean and how extensive is it?

- Since the part of us that has this experience separates from the body to the extent that it does, is that not an indication that not only do we have a soul, but that we are a soul resident in a manifested life form? If that is true, what else is true about life, about death, about soul, about purpose and mission and Source and Creation?

We may not be observing the emergence of a new species because of the aftereffects of incidents like near-death so much as witnessing the dynamics of species adaptation at work. And what better time than now? The positive results of the near-death experience exactly model what people need to strive for if the demands of the global community/marketplace are to be successfully met.

At this juncture in near-death research, it is obvious that confining investigations to a single hospital or to a single region of the country no longer serves the purpose it once did. My work and that of others illustrates that there are regionalisms, culturalisms, and religiousisms that overlay the imagery found in near-death scenarios, not to mention how the aftereffects are interpreted and dealt with. Nothing short of a multidisciplinary investigation of international scope will now suffice.

Validation for NDErs?

Let me be clear here: No amount of research can ever validate the near-death experience; only the one who had it can. Nevertheless, near-death research can unveil dimensions to the human body and mind, interrelationships between people, and the impact of individual belief systems on life and death experiences that may indeed challenge the very foundation of what society currently accepts as true and valid. Not only can near-death research do this, it must.

Amazing stories from transformed individuals carry us only so far. Only when we can truly affect surgical methodologies, nursing and hospice care, understandings of brain development, faculty extension training programs, and the philosophical underpinnings of individual and group belief systems will the near-death phenomenon deliver the real message it has to offer.

PMH Atwater: Internationally renowned NDE researcher and author. She earned a doctorate in humanities from the International College of Spiritual and Psychical Studies in Montreal, Canada, in 1992, and she has served on the board of the International Association for Near-Death Studies.

FATE February 1995

NEAR DEATH AND OUT OF THE BODY
Christopher Bloom

When Raymond Moody brought the phenomenon of the near-death experience to public attention in 1975, the skeptics quickly put up their guard. They argued that such "fantasies" were inconsequential.

They had a harder time dealing with University of Connecticut psychologist Kenneth Ring who demonstrated a few years later that these episodes are commonly reported by people who have survived clinical death. Now the skeptics argued that these vivid out-of-body experiences were either hallucinations caused by lack of oxygen to the brain or sophisticated episodes of depersonalization through which the experiencers try to deny what is happening to them.

Finally, however, the skeptics are going to have to admit defeat, for new evidence documenting the near-death experience has come to light, data that can't be explained away by any catch-all psychological or neurophysiological theory. This documentation has been accumulated by Dr. Michael Sabom, a pleasant, soft-spoken cardiologist associated with the Atlanta Veterans' Administration Medical Center who also serves as an assistant professor of medicine at Emory University.

Sabom has been investigating the NDE since May 1976 and completed his major research project in 1981. At first, he was primarily interested in reports filed by cardiac patients at the hospitals in which he worked but soon began pursuing reports from other sources. He eventually completed 116 interviews. He was singularly impressed when he found that some of his cardiac patients and other witnesses actually *watched* their operations or resuscitations during their NDEs. It struck him that many of these informants had seen and accurately described events that were well beyond the medical knowledge of the average layman. This first came to Sabom's attention in 1977 soon after he initiated his research project.

A 52-year-old night watchman, a Floridian with a history of heart problems, was admitted to the University of Florida's medical center in November 1977 for cardiac catheterization and subsequent surgery. Sabom was still in training at the hospital at the time and was able to do a complete follow-up on the case. The patient had undergone an NDE during a previous operation and experienced a second out-of-body experience in January 1978 during open-heart surgery.

The watchman's NDE was fairly typical. He reported that he lost consciousness during the operation but was now viewing the entire proceedings from a point about two feet above his body. From this vantage point he could look right down at what was happening. He described the sensation as "like I was another person in the room." He watched the two doctors work on him and stitch him up after the operation. His unique out-of-body perspective enabled him to make detailed observations of the surgery itself. On two occasions during the operation he saw one of the doctors plunge a syringe into his heart, once on each side. He also noticed that a sheet covered his head and was surprised that the lighting in the room was dim and diffused.

The watchman was also surprised by the appearance of his heart during surgery.

"They had all kinds of instruments stuck in the aperture," he recalled when Sabom interviewed him. "I think they're called clamps, clamps all over the place. I was amazed that I had thought there would be blood all over the place but there really wasn't much blood… and the heart doesn't look like I thought it did. It's big. And this is after the doctor had taken little pieces of it off. It's not shaped like I thought it

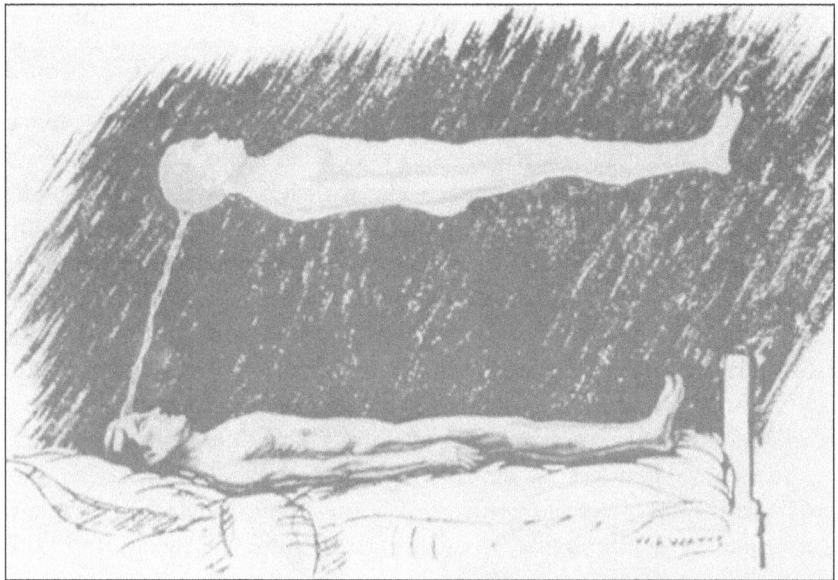

Separation of the astral body from the physical body, connected by the etheric cord. From The Projection of the Astral Body *by Hereward Carrington and Sylvan Muldoon, 1929.*

would be. My heart was shaped something like the continent of Africa... bean-shaped is another way you would describe it. Maybe mine is odd-shaped... [The surface was] pinkish and yellow. I thought the yellow area was fat tissue or something. Yucky, kind of. One general area to the right or left was darker than the rest instead of all being the same color."

The watchman became engrossed in observing the open-heart surgery and listened as his doctors discussed the procedures they were contemplating or implementing. They discussed a bypass, examined a swollen vein and twisted his heart around the better to examine it. The patient even noticed that one of the physicians was wearing patent leather shoes and another had a small blood clot under one fingernail.

Intrigued by this report and his interview with the watchman, Sabom obtained the files on the case and read the surgeon's report. He found that the patient's description represented an amazingly accurate layman's description of the procedures used during his surgery. A self-retaining retractor had been used, the patient had suffered an aneurysm which discolored part of his heart and the heart had been twisted around during the procedure. Even the syringe he had seen inserted had played a role; it had been used twice to remove air from his heart.

The technical detail included in the watchman's report particularly impressed the Georgia physician. It seems unlikely that an unsophisticated layman could be familiar with such detail and this made it seem that the NDE might represent a more significant phenomenon than most doctors had hitherto considered it to be.

Dr. Sabom's curiosity was further piqued when he studied the case of a Missouri woman who had undergone lumbar disk surgery in 1972. She too had witnessed her operation while out of her body and later described it accurately. A cogent aspect of this case involved the chief resident's participation in the operation when the woman had been led to believe that her physician-in-attendance would be playing the crucial role. Only later did she learn that the chief resident had directed the surgery, and although she had never met him, she recognized him immediately when she saw him during her recovery.

With such cases as these on file, Sabom soon found himself actively pursuing near-death survivors' reports in which they describe the medical procedures used during their operations and resuscitations. These reports have come primarily from patients in cardiac arrest, Sabom's own specialty. He believes that if cardiac arrest patients' observations prove accurate, these very special cases will do much to document the authenticity of the near-death experience. The cardiologist has now collected some 32 cases of individuals who saw their own bodies during their NDEs and six cardiac arrest victims in particular who have recalled specific and accurate details of their resuscitations. This isn't a great number, but their quality makes up for their sparse number.

One case Dr. Sabom investigated was that of a 60-year-old housewife who had been hospitalized for back strain. Sitting in her hospital bed, she apparently had a heart attack and lost consciousness. Regaining consciousness moments later, she found herself at the side of her bed watching the efforts being made to revive her. A nurse rushed to her inert body and a team of attendants began working on her, punching her chest, inserting an IV, giving her an injection, checking for a pulse and examining her eyes. While out of her body the patient also noted the equipment the attendants were using. She saw what she called a "breathing machine" and "a cart with a whole bunch of stuff on it." This cart stood beside the one bearing the IV equipment. She also overheard the doctor tell the nurse that she (the patient) must be rushed to the intensive care unit, and the woman watched as her belongings were taken from drawers and stuffed into bags and suitcases.

When Sabom interviewed this woman, he concentrated on her description of the equipment cart and asked if the doctors had taken any instruments from it. The woman replied that they hadn't but added, "... the breathing thing they put on my face. It was just a cone-shaped thing that went over my nose. When the doctor was pushing on my chest, they had this on me. They didn't leave it on very long... I guess they thought it was useless."

To validate this patient's experience, Sabom contacted the hospital where she had been treated and read the report on the emergency. The record confirmed everything the woman had reported, although she had never had access to the hospital report. He concluded that her description of the cardiac resuscitation was "extremely realistic from a medical point of view: the starting of an IV, external cardiac massage, the administration of oxygen by mask, the checking of carotid pulsations and pupillary response and the gathering and labeling of personal effects."

Sabom didn't stop there. He was also curious about the woman's claim that she had been given an injection right at the start of the cardiopulmonary resuscitation (CPR) attempt. The hospital's medical report documented this as well: the patient had been given an injection of concentrated glucose in case her coma was a result of low blood sugar.

An even more vivid description of a cardiac arrest resuscitation came from a 46-year-old laborer who lived in a small town in Georgia. He had gone into cardiac arrest after a heart attack in January 1978. He was hospitalized at the time and while out of his body he watched the steps taken to save his life. Sabom interviewed this man in January 1979 when the events were still fresh in his mind. The patient had vivid memories not only of the NDE but also of the events that led up to it.

"I thought I was getting sick," he told the cardiologist at the beginning of their conversation. "I got up on the side of the bed and heaved – and that's the last thing I remember until I was floating right up on the ceiling."

The patient then saw his body lying in bed; its sides were still up. He saw his wife and his doctor there and a third person whom he didn't recognize. His wife was crying but the laborer's attention was focused not on her but on the attempts being made to save him. He watched passively as a nurse with a defibrillation machine placed the pads on his body ("them shocker things," he called them). His body jumped almost a foot when the electrical charge was sent through his body and the shock aborted his out-of-body experience. He felt as if he had been forced back to his body and pushed into it.

Sabom pressed the man for more details about the use of the defibrillation paddles which had been so instrumental in saving his life. The man explained that he had seen the nurse rubbing the pads and that she had turned on the current by flipping a switch at the right-hand side of the apparatus to which the paddles were connected. Everyone was warned to stand clear.

Once again Sabom checked hospital records to document the accuracy of the patient's report. The cardiologist was especially impressed by the patient's description of the defibrillation paddles because he had mentioned certain procedures associated with their use which are familiar only to persons with medical training. The paddles are spread with a lubricant and routinely touched together, just as the patient said, to spread it evenly for maximum skin contact. The patient had also correctly designated just where on his body the paddles had been placed.

The patient had seen his weeping wife in the room and Sabom also interviewed her about the emergency. She verified her husband's account, saying that she had seen him vomit right before he became unconscious. She had started to cry only after she thought her husband was unaware of what was happening.

The patient's wife was flabbergasted by the whole affair – especially when her husband told her what he had seen after he had apparently lost consciousness. His recollections, she told Sabom, matched what she recalled of the scene and the attempts to get his heart beating again. "I thought if you were unconscious, you really didn't know what's going on," she said.

Through these investigations, Dr. Sabom became more and more convinced that the near-death experience cannot be dismissed as hallucination or a dream – but he was plagued by a lingering doubt. Could these patients be fantasizing or dreaming about what a cardiac resuscitation might entail? Since some of his star witnesses had undergone more than one heart attack, he considered it a real possibility that they might know something about cardiac resuscitation from reading, exposure to television shows such as *Medical Center*, or exposure to CPR techniques and medical equipment through earlier hospital experiences. Most of his witnesses denied having any such knowledge, but Sabom was far from sure that they couldn't have picked it up quite unintentionally.

To investigate this possibility, Sabom began to interview seasoned cardiac patients about their familiarity with standard CPR techniques. Some of these patients had undergone open-heart surgery, elective cardioversion or heart attacks which entailed various forms of treatment. Most of them had at least had the opportunity to observe the use of standard cardiac monitors, defibrillators and other such equipment. Each patient was asked to imagine that he or she was watching a medical team reviving a heart arrest victim and to describe the procedure in as much detail as possible. These interviews were tape-recorded and then analyzed.

The results were nothing short of amazing. Just about every one of the patients described the procedures incorrectly.

Their most common error reflected the widespread belief that mouth-to-mouth resuscitation would be attempted. It is rarely used in hospitals because more effective methods are readily available. The patients also tended to misunderstand the way a victim's air passage might be cleared and were confused about cardiac massage and electrical defibrillation. Only three of Sabom's control patients gave reasonably accurate descriptions of some CPR procedures, but even these accounts were not precise. Sabom concluded that in general even seasoned heart patients have little idea of what is involved in reviving a cardiac arrest victim. Their conjectures, he noted, were certainly far less accurate than the accounts of those persons who have watched these procedures while out of their bodies. As a result, Sabom doesn't hold with the idea that people who have experienced NDEs are only "dreaming" about their resuscitations or drawing their information from prior exposure to CPR techniques. "Some other explanation must be sought to explain these findings," he says.

The case of a retired air force pilot demonstrates the fact that medical observations made by near-death survivors can be incredibly detailed. The Florida airman had suffered a massive heart attack one day in 1973 and the next day, while recovering in a hospital, he went into cardiac arrest, apparently while he was asleep. He found himself standing beside his body as a team of attendants rushed into the room. His description of how they revived him contained extraordinary detail.

"The first thing they did," he said, "was put an injection into the IV, the rubber gasket they have there for pushes. I was getting a lot of lidocaine… pushes because I had an arrhythmia. Then they lifted me up and moved me onto the plywood. That's when [the doctor] began to do the pounding on the chest and it didn't hurt, though it cracked a rib. I felt no pain."

Next came the administration of oxygen which the patient heard and saw accurately.

"They had oxygen on me before," he continued, "one of those little nose tubes, and they took that off and put on a face mask which covers your mouth and nose. It was a type of pressure thing. I remember instead of oxygen just being there it was hissing like under pressure. Seems someone was holding that thing most of the time."

He further described it as "sort of a soft plastic mask, light green color." It was attached to a hose leading to the oxygen. He also recalled the use of the defibrillator; he had watched its meter with rapt attention. The meter, he explained, was square with two needles. A nurse set one in a fixed position and the other moved up and down the scale. This second needle "seemed to come up rather slowly," he recalled. "It didn't just pop up like a meter or a voltmeter or something registering." The first needle remained preset and the patient described the other rising higher and higher on the meter before each successive jolt of electricity was applied to his body. He concluded his account with a detailed description of the defibrillator itself and the application of its paddles to his body.

Sabom was amazed by the pilot's account. His description of the CPR procedures was accurate and his account of the needles and their movement was uncannily precise, certainly beyond the scope of anyone who has not had personal experience with a defibrillator and has not been trained in its use. The meters on machines used in the 1970s did indeed have two needles. One remained stable; it was used to preselect the amount of electricity to be discharged. The other needle indicated that the machine was being charged up to the selected amount and thus it moved gradually up the meter. More modern models, designed without the meter, are now in use but the pilot's recollections were totally consistent with the machine in use at the time of his cardiac arrest.

Is it possible that the pilot had seen such an instrument in operation at some previous time? Sabom thinks this is unlikely. The patient denied having any familiarity with the apparatus and he tended to downplay the importance of his experience. To this day the former cardiac patient insists it was not unusual!

"It hasn't changed my thinking about life, death, the hereafter or anything else," he told Sabom.

The former air force pilot has no vested interest in using his experience to prove anything and it therefore seems unlikely that he would deliberately lie about it to make it sound impressive.

The cases summarized here represent only a few of many similar incidents Dr. Sabom has collected. These incidents all point to the fact that persons who undergo NDEs during cardiac arrest – or any other medical emergency – really are aware of what is happening to them, what procedures are being used to revive them, who is caring for them and what is being said by the attending medical staff. Subsequent research by Sabom and his colleagues has also demonstrated that the technical level of what patients see and hear is well above the base-level information most people have about standard CPR techniques.

Dr. Sabom's research is probably the most important line of evidence showing that the NDE cannot be dismissed as a quirk of the brain, hallucination resulting from lack of oxygen or some obscure psychological anomaly. Sabom also rejects the possibility that these reports can be accounted for as subconscious fabrications, endorphic release in the brain, temporal lobe seizures or any other physiological manifestation. All the evidence suggests that these events are precisely what they are reported to be: the release of awareness from the body resulting from a close brush with death.

Could the NDE represent the first stages of the release of the soul from the body? Dr. Sabom isn't sure. "As a physician and scientist," he concludes in his book *Recollections of Death*, "I cannot, of course, say for sure that the NDE is indicative of what is to come at the moment of final bodily death. These experiences were encountered during waning moments of life. Those [persons] reporting these experiences were not brought back from the dead but were rescued from a point very close to death. Thus, in the strictest sense, these experiences are encounters of near-death and not of death itself. Since I suspect that the NDE is a reflection of a mind-brain split, I cannot help wondering why such an event should occur at the point of near-death. Could the mind which splits apart from the physical brain be, in essence, the 'soul,' which continues to exist after final bodily death, according to some religious doctrines?"

FATE February 1984

RETURN FROM DEATH
Ronald L. Voreis

During the Vietnam war I was an Air Force pilot flying the gunship version of the C-130, the AC-130. This was a big airplane, a four-engine turbojet with 105mm cannons and the latest in electronic/laser-guided fire power. We flew only at night, usually after midnight. The stress of being at war, being shot at and trying to sleep irregular hours was sometimes unbearable. I, like everyone else, was taking it just a day at a time. With so many unknowns you never knew what tomorrow might bring.

It was the spring of 1971. Somehow, I'd made it through the first nine months and I was overdue for a working R & R (rest and relaxation). We were given this working vacation halfway into our 18-month tour of duty. It would take us out of the primary war zone to an adjacent country, away from the normal stresses. My crew and I were sent to Thailand, to fly local resupply and personnel transport missions in the standard cargo version of the C-130.

Our air base was situated just outside of Utapao, a beautiful little tropical township along the ocean in south Thailand. The beaches were long and sandy with rippling sand dunes. It was the perfect place to kick back and unwind a little from the war.

With this sudden release from tension and anxiety, something peculiar happened to me. The body, when stressed, can operate on hidden reserves for extended periods, but when the crisis is removed, it's time to pay the piper. I believe this is what led to my almost fatal heart attack.

Behind the aircraft

We had been there about two days. On this particular day, it all began pretty much as usual. After briefing for a 6 AM takeoff, checking the route and weather, we boarded the airplane and started our preflight checks. I was feeling well, but I noticed the pace of my checklist routine seemed slow and too methodical. My brain and my body were out of sync for some reason. We took off and headed for our first destination. I really felt "behind the aircraft." (In pilot lingo this is a condition which could put your airplane and the lives of your crew in serious jeopardy.) You have to be extra aware when this happens and mentally cross-check everything you do. It's helpful too that another pilot is sitting next to you.

Thankfully it was a short mission, and we were back at home base in five hours. It was lunchtime and keeping with normal routine we set out for the Officer's Club. After five hours in an airplane you're somewhat dehydrated, a little smelly and very hungry. We all wore flight suits, so no one seemed overly offensive to another. I ordered the steak dinner and had a bottle of beer. We talked about going into town to see a strip show and continue drinking, but something was wrong. I could actually feel my blood pressure rising inside – at least that's what I thought it was.

Into another reality

The guys went on into town and I excused myself with some half lie about needing to study for an upgrade test. You never admitted to being sick, especially not to crew members.

I walked slowly back to the B.O.Q. room. That strange pressure was still building inside, but an alarming dull pain was growing in my chest too. After what seemed like an awfully long walk, I entered the room and sat down sluggishly on the bed. I began to lose my balance, and I fell sideways across the bed, my feet still dangling over the side.

Ronald L. Vorais

It's important to note that I was fully aware of everything, every moment. At no time did I lose consciousness. A strong vibration suddenly gripped my heart. It wasn't as painful as it was alarming, but the thought of a heart attack crossed my mind. The vibration became stronger. I felt my heart stop and begin to quiver.

Then my conscious self – my total awareness – started to shrink. From my head, my fingers and my toes, the full circumference of my awareness began shrinking into a tight little ball centered in my heart. All the while I was amazed, not believing what was happening, but thinking that somehow, I must be dying.

And the pain began. It wasn't what we normally feel as pain. It was a mixture of pain and ecstasy so delicate and rare it might better be termed "rapture."

Centered there in my heart, I (my conscious being) began a deep, instinctive struggle to break free. I perceived myself encompassed in a cocoon of gauzy fibers: a womb that was now my heart. I flashed back to my birth and realized the similarity. An unseen hand, so gentle but persistent, gave me an assist. I sensed being strained through stringy fibers, being pushed through with an urgency hard to explain. The process was being guided, and I had little control over whatever was happening.

Finally, the gauze broke and I shot out like a cannonball! I found myself floating in the air, floating among fluffy clouds. I expected to see angels. I had such a joyous, free feeling; all cares and worries were left behind, my mind was clearer than I ever remembered, and I felt I had access to any knowledge I cared to explore.

I looked down, and surprise of surprises, the airbase and the city of Utapao lay below me exactly as I had seen them from the air during landing. My reaction gradually waned to, "Oh well," but my excitement with my new condition was hard to contain. I knew that other curiosities lay ahead, so I flew through the air doing loops and spins, dives and climbs – everything you could do in an airplane, but better.

I remember thinking, "So this is what it's like to die. Why did I ever fear it? If people could only know." I pinched myself to be sure I was really awake, and sure enough I felt it. Taking a closer look at what I pinched, my skin was fleshy and real, though softer with a pink translucence.

Far ahead in the distance I noticed a dark but strangely beautiful rain cloud growing into a giant thunderstorm. Gold rays glistened around its edges, giving it an aura of golden light. It was the most noble-looking, exotic cloud I'd ever seen. The more I looked, the more enchanted I became. My attention on it seemed to draw me to it. Slowly at first, then with growing attraction, like magnetism, I flew almost uncontrolled into its center.

Inside, an explosion of colors and rippling electrical sensations danced in, on, around and through me. There is no way to describe it. Words do not suffice. I heard a voice. It was soft, caring and melodious. It told me many things, but you know, to this day I don't remember what was said or what was told me. It may have been in a different language, or it may have been blocked from my conscious mind. I don't know.

I sensed there was a doorway there too, an entry into the next world. But it would not yet be for me because unexpectedly, I tumbled out of the bottom of this glorious cloud. I saw the familiar little town of Utapao below me again and I just floated down, landing feet first on a busy street.

I walked swiftly to the sidewalk. The smell of raw fish and fresh vegetables wafted the air from the open markets. Busy little Thai people darted from shop to market greeting others but taking no notice of me. I wondered if they could see or sense me in any way. "Wouldn't it be great to be invisible?" I thought.

A man approached me. He was apparently deep in thought, and his eyes stared far ahead. I reached out and touched my hand to his shoulder (his body felt soft and spongy to my touch), but he showed no response. I was indeed invisible, but oddly I could see and hear and smell and touch all that they could – maybe more! I walked in and out (yes, even through) several of the shops, just browsing, totally enjoying my unique circumstance, quite invisible to the rest of the world.

At some point I heard the familiar drone of engines from one of our own planes. It had just taken off from the base and I looked up to watch it climb. As before, my attention on it drew me like a magnet and I found myself floating up to meet it. I'd never seen a plane in the air from this perspective. I flew alongside, slipping in and out of the jet wash, tumbling backwards at times like a bird caught in the terrific vortex currents.

It occurred to me to take a peek inside the cockpit, just to see if I recognized who was flying. My desire propelled me there, almost effortless, and I peered in at the two pilots as they dutifully scanned instruments and horizon in the prescribed manner. I could see their heads and eyes, but their faces remained out of focus. I tried to refocus, but something blocked my clear view of their features.

With an abrupt painful SLAP, I landed back in my body. The impact made me sting all over. I opened my eyes, sat straight up and exclaimed, "My God!" My astonishment with the whole episode had dawned on me fully.

What I had gone through was an out-of-body experience, but later I realized it was also called a near-death experience. The two are synonymous in my opinion and only a step away from that lasting separation of body and spirit. Why some come back from this borderland state is a mystery, but I suspect it has something to do with unfinished business, or a drastic change in life plan.

This single experience had a dramatic impact on me. My personal life and goals took a big turn afterwards. I lost all ambition to make the military my permanent career. In fact, I felt a strong urge to go into the field of psychology instead (which I ultimately did). My values changed from self-serving to other-serving.

But also, I would never fear death again. I would never again doubt the separate existence of the self or spirit from the body. The spirit has a body of its own, and a place of its own, a place of beauty and joys beyond belief. This is our natural state of being, and our birthright to return to when we've finished here.

Your experience of death will probably not be the same as mine. I think that our Lord, or Higher Self, greets us back home in different ways, depending on the state of our consciousness and the degree of our understanding of Truth. But whatever the way, it will be meaningful, and it will be beautiful.

FATE July 1991

MEN WHO CAME BACK FROM THE DEAD
Edmund P. Gibson

There are living persons whose hearts have stopped beating, whose respiration has ceased, and who have been declared dead by medical men. They have later revived and been able to tell of their experiences. The number is not large. Some have had little to say of their adventure with death. Either nothing occurred, or upon awakening they did not remember their experiences.

Those who return from the dead and do remember their "out of the body" adventures have an interesting story to tell. These stories substantiate in some degree the stories told by returning personalities in Spiritualist seances.

Some years ago, Mr. C. Uxkull was visiting in Kazan, Russia. He was taken to the hospital there, suffering with severe pneumonia. At the time of his crisis he was placed under an oxygen bag which covered his face. As he lost consciousness he suddenly found himself standing beside the group of hospital officials and attendants, looking down on his own body.

He tried to touch the doctor but failed. He tried to touch right hand to left and found that his hands passed through each other. Uxkull found that he could walk along the floor, but he could no longer feel the floor. He again tried to touch the doctor, but his hand was stopped at a distance of about an inch and he could not bring it closer to the doctor's body. All of this time, he was conscious of his body lying on the cot before him, sometimes in full view, sometimes obscured by the movements of the nurses. Throughout this experience he had a feeling of lightness, as though buoyed up by the surrounding air.

Uxkull tried to speak to his physician, but he could not make himself heard. He felt that the body in which he was standing was solid, despite the strange phenomenon he had observed with his hands. He tried to attract attention but could not.

At this moment, Uxkull became conscious that the group watching his recumbent figure on the cot was breaking up. The doctor pronounced him dead. This disturbed him since he knew that he was still alive and walking beside the nurses and orderlies. He stood beside an old Russian nurse as she gave the death blessing to his body, lying before him.

As the body was being moved to the morgue Uxkull became conscious of two spirits or angels who took him by the arms and led him out of the ward. They guided him through the wall and into the street. They walked in a blinding snowstorm which Uxkull could see but could not feel. Then he and his conductors ascended swiftly into space. He was among a swarm of space creatures. They seemed to be evil spirits who tried to separate him from his guides. His guides took him still higher. Here was a sphere of intense, blinding white light, so intense that he was conscious only of the light. He heard a majestic voice pronounce that he was not ready.

He lost consciousness and awoke outside the hospital wall. His two guides were still with him. They again led him through the walls of the building and into the morgue where he saw his body stretched upon a mortuary table. His sister knelt crying beside the body. Then Uxkull suddenly felt terribly cold and damp and awoke within his physical body. His sister was still beside him. He lost consciousness again and later awoke in the hospital ward, surrounded by a group of hospital attendants. Beside him stood the chief surgeon, who earlier had pronounced him dead.

This story of Uxkull's death and revival was written by him and published in the *Moscow Journal*. An American translation was made by Basil Doudine who published it under the title: *My Death and Revival* by C. Uxkull.

In April 1935, Dr. G. B. Kirkland, British medical officer in Southern Rhodesia, explained a post-mortem experience to a meeting of the International Institute for Psychical Research.

"After a long series of desperate operations, grave-faced doctors stood beside my bed and pronounced that I could not possibly live through the night. At one o'clock in the morning I officially died and remained in suspended animation for some time.

"Suddenly, to my intense surprise, I saw myself lying upon my back. The thought flashed through me that I did not think much of me – in fact I did not approve of me at all. Almost before this thought had time to materialize, I found myself and others, very faintly discernible, in a tunnel like a railway tunnel with a speck of light at the end.

"These others were all hurrying along as fast as they could but did not seem to make much headway. It was terribly cold, and I kept putting around myself some gray garments, which did not keep out the cold. After a long struggle I managed to get into a fairly good stride and the cold was not so great. It was beginning to feel better and the light was gradually getting brighter.

"Then someone or something flashed up in front of me and blotted out the light. Instantly I was in a terrible struggle. In the middle of the struggle everything went black, and the next thing I knew I was alive again."

Dr. Kirkland believes that he made a post-mortem visit to some sort of "astral hell." His visit was terminated by his revival though he had been declared dead by the attending physician.

In Arley, England, on February 8, 1935, John Puckering, a market gardener, lay dead upon the operating table. For four and one-half minutes his heart was still and he did not breathe. The attending surgeon opened the chest cavity and massaged his heart. Puckering revived. The doctor said that he made the chest incision "more from a sense of duty than with any hope." However, the old gardener's heart responded and Puckering regained consciousness.

Puckering said that he was sorry that they had brought him back. "What I saw during my brief spell of death makes me regret I ever came back," he said.

He told reporters he had found himself surrounded by thousands of happy people. Three of them he recognized, and he realized he must be among the dead. He found his wife, who had died the year before.

He appeared truly disappointed to be back again.

"The grave has no terrors for me now. I realize that earthly life, sorrowful as it can be, is just a training ground for something fuller and better," he said.

FATE November 1950

MY JOURNEY INTO LIGHT
Douglas DeLong

The lights were dim in the intensive care unit of the local hospital. The small nursing staff of the night shift was on duty. I was lying in a bed directly across from the nursing station. Several tubes had been inserted into my body; one in the upper left side of my chest, one into a nostril, another into the left side of my abdomen and a fourth one into the wrist. Two of these originated from IV bottles and the other two ran back into drainage machines.

Surgical mishap
It was here that I was recovering from major bowel surgery. In fact, this was the second "bowel resection" for me in less than a week. Earlier that day, I had been reopened with a knife from above my groin to just below the sternum. Heavy sutures and clamping devices resembling large hair curlers had been used to close the new incision. Unfortunately, several hours later some of the sutures burst open, exposing my intestinal tract.

The pain was unbearable already, but with this further mishap it became excruciating. (Upon reflection, I can honestly say that I know what the pain of childbirth feels like for most women, although I am a man!) I drifted in and out of consciousness throughout the day. When I became lucid, I would beg the nurses for a pain killer, anything to ease the agony. Each time I was informed gently that my heart was beating too slowly to receive any morphine or Demerol for relief.

At 19 years of age, I thought I had my whole life ahead of me and that this nightmare should not be happening. It was very difficult to comprehend all of this. The only thing l understood was the terrible pain.

A male nurse was one of the night staff. He was sitting at the nursing station across from me reading something. l was now in a clearer state of mind and could observe him and the surrounding area of the intensive care unit as I lay there. It was at that moment l felt a strange tug in my solar plexus. This sensation became stronger.

Then my awareness moved down from my eyes to my solar plexus. From there I felt myself floating out of my pain-wracked body. Once I was completely free of my physical form, the pain disappeared.

Floating above

I could see everything around me in great detail. This included the thin, emaciated person lying below me in the hospital bed. His eyes were shut, and he appeared to be in a deep sleep or even dead.

I realized that I was now gazing at my own body. It resembled a wax figure. Although this gave me an eerie feeling for a second, it quickly ceased.

I became more curious and started to float across the room toward the nursing station where the male nurse was sitting. l floated effortlessly over him and looked down at what he was reading; it was the sports section of the local newspaper. For some reason, he was unaware of my presence. A strong reading lamp shone directly onto him and his reading material. This same light seemed to shine right through me.

After a brief moment, I continued with my exploration. I felt free as a bird in flight as I drifted around the corner of the nursing station toward three glass cubicles situated immediately behind. The center cubicle contained a bed with a sick, elderly man in it. He had recently suffered from a heart attack. A pillow propped him up as he rested with

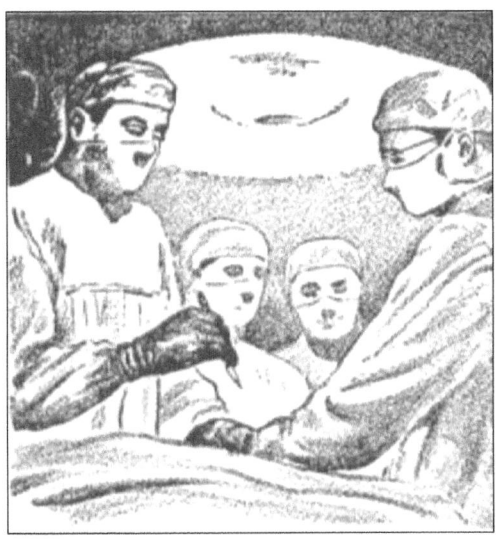
Surgery complications led one man to a near-death experience.

his eyes closed. I entered his room or cubicle and floated above him. As I did that, he opened his eyes, smiled and waved at me. I waved back at him. This seemed strange. The nurse had not seen me nor been aware of my presence. Yet this deathly ill man could see me in my soul form. He had even communicated with me in some way. The next day, this poor fellow passed away.

After that, I went down the small corridor, around to the other side of the nursing station. I headed toward the double doors that led out of the intensive care unit. The doors may have been closed, but I passed right through them like a ghost. I moved down the quiet hospital hallway and veered to the left. I continued along this hallway until l reached a steel door that was off to my left. The word "morgue" was written on the front of the door. As before, I went right through the door. I was now floating within a cold, sterile room. The floor had a granite stone look to it. The wall in front of me contained several freezer doors. The scene reminded me of a murder mystery where someone has to go to the morgue to identify the body.

I felt very uncomfortable here and wanted to leave right away. As soon as I thought this, I started to fly rapidly up through the ceiling and through the roof of the hospital. I shot up into the night sky like a Roman candle. My soul continued upward into space. Soon I was moving along at an incredible speed. Many stars seemed to flow past me. It looked like an episode of *Star Trek* when the starship goes into warp drive.

The tunnel of light
Then my soul started to slow down as I spotted a beautiful white light ahead. Instantly I was standing, or more accurately floating, in front of this intense, vivid light. I experienced a sense of peace here. This light was actually a long tunnel with even more light radiating from deep within the center. I felt an overwhelming urge to enter into the tunnel toward the radiance at the far end. The sensation of being home filled my being. I felt comfort and joy in this wonderful place as I floated down the long tunnel.

Up ahead I started to see people looking toward me. They were faint but discernible. There was a blue sky in the background. All the people felt very familiar.

It was at this point that two beings of light appeared on each side of me. Their ethereal hands reached out and gently touched me. My forward momentum stopped, even though I wished to continue traveling toward this scene.

These two light bodies or angels began to talk. Neither one of the angels spoke verbally. Instead, the words and messages given to me came in a telepathic form. I could hear their voices inside my head clearly. They took turns talking. I was told repeatedly that it was not my time to go and that I had things to do on earth. The angel to the right of me stressed that I had an "arrangement with heaven" and needed to fulfill it. Both these ethereal beings radiated intense love and understanding toward me in my soul form.

Then a vision was shown to me. It was like watching television as the scenes unfolded. Future world events flashed before me in quick succession. Terrifying diseases, natural calamities, and major earth changes rolled across the screen. Just before the vision came to an end, a final scene was shown. This one was of a more positive nature. It involved a world embracing spirituality and love. The impression was that earth and heaven would be closer to each other. Angels and other spiritual beings would work together with people on earth in the near future.

When this prophetic vision ended, the two angels smiled. They gently turned me away from the brilliant light and nudged my soul in the other direction. Soon, I was flying at an incredible speed past the stars. My soul continued in this manner until a beautiful blue planet came into sight. I shot down through the clouds until I was directly over the top of the local hospital. Then I went into the building itself and floated down into the intensive care unit.

There was an apprehension inside as I floated toward my almost lifeless body. I positioned myself in my soul essence right above the physical body. The face still looked pale and sickly. I started to move closer to the inert body, even though I was trying to fight this movement. I sensed that the hands and feet of my soul form were trying to keep me from descending into the body. Despite all my efforts, I slipped back into my physical form. It felt like cold clay as I settled within.

Back on Earth
In less than a second, I opened my eyes, fully awake. The intense pain was now back, so I pressed the call buzzer situated on the pillow beside my head. The male nurse heard the sound, looked up at me, and put down his newspaper. He came across to my bed very quickly, carrying a blood pressure machine. A stethoscope was hung about his neck. In a very expert and caring way, he checked my blood pressure and listened to my heartbeat. A slight smile came onto his face as he did this. He then looked down at me with kindness and said, "Your heartbeat and breathing are stronger. I can give you something for the pain now."

With that, he gave me an injection of Demerol that eased the pain in a few minutes. I knew at that moment that I would survive the ordeal. There would be a few rough times ahead, but I would overcome them and live a productive life. With that thought in mind, I drifted off into a pleasant sleep.

I look back upon my near-death experience as a journey into light. Once I became healed, some special abilities started to re-manifest. As a child, I could see auras or energy around people and things. Visitations by angels and spirit guides were common occurrences for me. After this profound experience at age 19, l started to see lights and then colors around people again. Soon I could see the human aura of everyone very distinctly. I was able to interpret accurately what the colors meant.

Most survivors of near-death experiences, or NDEs, develop an intense desire to seek a spiritual path. Many will do so through means other than organized religion. A deeper understanding and appreciation of life can be the result. Some survivors develop special psychic and spiritual gifts. For them, the small dramas of life become less important than the greater life plan they have been shown.

Douglas DeLong: Author of Ancient Teachings for Beginners, *spiritual teacher, past-life therapist, chakra master, and medical intuitive, co-founder with his wife, Carol, of the DeLong Ancient Mystery School in Saskatoon, Canada.*

FATE September 2003

A CLOSER LOOK AT BETTY EADIE'S NEAR-DEATH EXPERIENCE
Scott S. Smith

Betty Eadie's *Embraced By the Light,* touted as "the most profound and complete near-death experience ever," with a foreword by major NDE author Melvin Morse, spent months on *The New York Times* bestseller list. There are a million copies in print, yet not much public awareness of its central secret.

Rehashing Mormon theology

It is obvious to anyone familiar with the teachings of the Church of Jesus Christ of Latter-day Saints, better known as the Mormons, that Betty Eadie's account is virtually a verbatim rehashing of the church's Doctrine and Covenants, which consists primarily of revelations to founding prophet Joseph Smith. Yet there is no acknowledgment of this in Eadie's book.

It is difficult to believe that this was not intentionally concealed, and yet anyone who knows Betty Eadie would agree that she is too honest and open to be deceptive. Her naiveté understandably strains one's credulity, however.

Responding to questions about this, she insists that Muslims think her book is Islamic, despite the fact that Christ is central to her story. Pressed further, she says that a Muslim who dies will be met by someone from his or her faith, but eventually everyone will have a chance to accept Christ (Mormons depart from mainstream Christianity in believing that everyone gets a chance to embrace Christ, here or on the other side). Eadie also asserts that Catholics think her book is Catholic, claiming that she does not herself think of the book as Mormon.

A Native American Mormon

After all, she says, while she had been baptized as a Mormon on the Lakota reservation when she was 21, she did so for non-religious reasons and knew little about the faith before her near-death experience a decade later. She saw no point in mentioning this in the book and says she simply could not have manufactured the details of her vision out of her cultural conditioning (she grew up going mainly to Baptist and Lutheran churches).

Besides, she points out, dozens of people have approached her to say they have had remarkably similar experiences, even though they are not Mormons. But no one, not even Eadie, seems to want to accept the implications.

While Eadie has managed to get this far with few noticing the Mormon aspect of the book, some of her fellow religionists have attacked her for taking too liberal a line about other faiths, pointing out that the Church of Jesus Christ of Latter-day Saints claims that it is the only gateway to the highest reaches of heaven (LDS theology postulates many levels in the hereafter).

The truth is somewhere in between their hard line and Eadie's attitude that she can preach Mormonism without being dogmatic about the implications. Early Mormon leaders taught that there was abundant truth in other religions, encouraging members to learn from other faiths, since the Mormon church inevitably would become contaminated with the secular cultures in which it found itself, and this was a way to get back to central truths (in fact, the current narrow-minded attitude is a new phenomenon in the church).

Still, even if one adopts Eadie's relaxed viewpoint, it is hard to keep a straight face when she tries to deflect questions about the Mormon theology behind her vision. It is like her comment that all religions are needed because everyone needs different steps on the ladder of truth.

But when pressed, she admits that anything that is "not good" (Satanism, the Branch Davidians) is not of God. And she grants that the book's notion that as people are ready for the truth they move up this religious ladder is an oversimplification. Just as often one could move down. She is a fluent proponent of a beautifully comprehensive and comforting vision that gets a little more complicated under scrutiny.

Although she says certain aspects of her experience were symbolic (seeing warriors in armor, for example), Eadie claims to have told everything exactly as she saw it, despite a lapse of two decades beyond the time she nearly expired from surgical complications in 1973. She attributes her ability to recall the four-hour NDE to a naturally excellent memory and God's will. She says she has remembered all of it consciously since the experience.

An extraordinary vision?

If so, it is the most extraordinary single vision ever recorded. No one, not Joseph Smith, Jesus Christ, the Apostle Paul nor Mohammed ever reported being told this much in one sitting. Why should she have a visitation to young Joseph that revealed to him the whereabouts of the plates on which the Book of Mormon was recorded?

Most outsiders assume that the Mormon scripture is sheer fantasy. The book was "translated" from metal plates supposedly hidden by an ancient American prophet, with Joseph Smith getting the English words by looking into "seer stones." Published in 1830, it tells a complex tale, which has gradually come to be backed by archaeological findings (see John Sorenson's *An Ancient American Setting for the Book of Mormon*, or Brigham Young University's *The Book of Mormon: The Keystone Scripture*, for example). Critics have simply not kept up with all the new developments.

That the Mormon scripture should have genuine historical backing bothers sophisticated critics for reasons different from those of a fundamentalist Christian viewpoint. William Bramwell, for example, uses a chapter in *The Gods of Eden* to raise an alarm about Mormonism as another example of the clever manipulation of earthly religious history by alien beings. He points to parallels between UFO abduction accounts and the angelic visitation to young Joseph that revealed to him the whereabouts of the plates on which the Book of Mormon was recorded.

Fastest growing major religion

But there is a Mormon response in the form of James Thompson's *Aliens & UFOs: Messengers or Deceivers?*, an analysis of the differences between Mormon supernatural experiences and those associated with UFOs, with a brilliant theory about a satanic intent behind the various elements of the standard abduction story.

Whatever side one takes in the debate, it shows that Mormonism has to be seriously considered as a contender for the claim to having the Truth, even though the church has less than 10 million people (it is, however, the fastest-growing major religion and seems to have influence well beyond its numbers, because of wealth and political power). Joseph Smith put together a theology whose central tenet is that anyone can become a god.

Unfortunately, it is presented in the context of an uninspiring culture that looks no more enlightened than fundamentalist Protestantism, and the vast anti-Mormon literature, despite being based on erroneous information, would scare off most students of things spiritual.

But one thing that stands out in Mormon culture is that it is full of supernatural experiences, and many of them are connected with the "work for the dead," which is tied to secretive temples. Talking to dead ancestors is not a rare event for Mormons. Neither are NDEs. Fundamentalist Christians would believe that this supernatural aspect of Mormonism as originating from satanic sources to provide credibility for this "wolf in sheep's clothing," to deceive true Christians. One does not have to buy into that particular conspiracy theory to see that the messages Betty Eadie was given are as satisfying initially as those of Betty Andreasson Luca, the subject of a series of books by Raymond Fowler about a celebrated UFO abductee. The aliens suggested to Luca that they were angels guarding the Earth, which fit in well with Luca's devout Christianity. As James Thompson notes in his Mormon analysis, however, the benevolent alien theory really does not hold up well under the microscope.

A comforting philosophy

The philosophy behind Eadie's book, as comforting and simple as Luca's, has to be weighed very carefully. Fundamentalist Mormons and Christians have allied themselves with a New Age philosophy which says that everything is meant to be. As soon as one challenges how that leaves us free will, proponents jump through verbal hoops to say that God is not forcing anyone to do anything.

But this ignores the fact that anything that can be predicted with 100 percent accuracy does not allow for true free will, which could change the outcome. Those who believe there is no conflict between prophecies, psychic predictions and free will do not understand the issues.

When Betty Eadie's assertion that we have free will gets challenged, she responds that we at least had it before we came here. Mormon doctrine maintains that we all lived a prior existence in the presence of God (Eadie says this and genetics explains reincarnation – this is inadequate, and there are better alternative explanations).

Eadie takes a position popular among Mormons, even though it is not church dogma, asserting that we pick our birth circumstances, a notion at home with Shirley MacLaine (they would agree that Holocaust victims chose their destiny). Eadie says the special spirits that choose to starve in Somalia or suffer from some disease of the eye in India are there to test our humanitarianism. When it is pointed out that few of us could be aware of most suffering, she asserts that it's a collective test of our state or church, not the individual.

Individual tests

But there are individual tests, too, and her book relates her NDE vision of a drunk whose spirit incarnated in order to test the charity of another man.

It is hard to see why this would be necessary, however, given the vast amount of drunkenness and every other problem that exists without some spirit deciding to add to the situation. And were all the actions of the man who ended up in the gutter just so much acting in the divine drama, rather than events worth taking seriously as expressions of choice, or a tragic lack of free will?

To Eadie's way of thinking, we choose our diseases to learn things (the Black Death was certainly popular). And we designed the rules of earth life, including the climate and weather extremes. To a query as to why we would have wanted to come to a place where virtually everyone spends his or her entire time just trying to physically survive, Eadie comments that everyone has different tastes.

"Some people love the arctic or the desert and they can't understand why I like rainy Seattle," is her observation. It seems odd that so much of the earth was made so difficult to live in (I guess I should be glad that not everyone had a preexistent taste for California, where I live).

Simplistic theories?

Like simplistic theories of karma, the ideas that we choose the circumstances of our birth and that we can reconcile free will with events "meant to be" provide more problems than they resolve, although few adherents of any comprehensive religious theories want to consider the philosophical challenges.

To the question of why pain needs to be as intense as it is in order to accomplish its apparent purpose in keeping us from mortally hurting ourselves, Betty Eadie has an easy answer: we differ in our tolerance of pain. She cites her father, who was hardly bothered by a heart attack.

On reflection, this is not satisfactory, like so many messages from beyond. It makes one wonder what is going on.

And one has to consider that the Tibetans also have a very elaborate explanation of what happens beyond the initial NDE stages, none of which fits with Eadie's vision. Unless one wants to fall into sloppy, if well-intended New Age thinking where all ways lead to the same goal, one has to face the fact that when reports conflict, not all of them can be right.

Unlike most NDErs, Eadie says she was given the option to stay on the other side (she believes we rarely go before our time, again bringing into question how much is a game of illusory free will). When she decided to return, she was given a mission to perform. It is not entirely the book, Eadie notes, because when she completes her mission, she was told she would die. But since her NDE, she has no fear of death.

Embraced By the Light explains why. Betty Eadie says she was told by God it would be a success long before it was published, and she picked an obscure non-Mormon publisher, Gold Leaf Press, because she was given divine guidance to do so.

But is she right about everything? Someone obviously wants us to think so.

If Betty Eadie is correct, her book should be regarded as one of the most important of our time.

FATE March 1994

NEAR-DEATH EXPERIENCES OF CHILDREN
PMH Atwater

Children of any age can have a near-death experience. That includes newborns and infants. What they describe, once they are able to verbalize, can be quite shocking to parents who are unfamiliar with the startling reality of near-death states.

With a research base of 277 child experiencers, I can say that the vast majority (76 percent) of children's scenarios are rather simple, featuring only three or fewer elements – things like loving, nothingness, friendly darkness, a special voice, an out-of-body experience, or a visitation of some kind. The closer the child is to puberty, the more apt he or she is to have a longer, more involved episode. Still, kids' cases run the gamut from hellish to heavenly, regardless of age. The youngest to have a terrifying experience was only nine days old. This baby girl was traumatized by ghoul-like beings who threatened her when she "died" during surgery. The event haunted her throughout her growing years until the age of 28, when she had a second near-death experience that explained the first one.

We all thrill to "out-of-the-mouth-of-babes" stories that inspire and uplift us, yet in our joy we fail to view what happened to the child from the child's eyes – nor are we alert for aftereffects.

Children's experiences

Don't let children's usually brief scenarios fool you – the key is intensity. In over two decades of research, I have found that it is the intensity of the experience, not necessarily the content, that has the greatest impact. The simplest episodes, if intense enough, engender the full range of psychological and physiological aftereffects – no matter the experiencer's age.

With that in mind, let's take a moment to compare child experiencers with adult experiencers. Remember, the intensity, and the aftereffects are the same, yet the different way kids deal with the phenomenon can be quite surprising.

Fifty-seven percent of child experiencers went on to enjoy long-lasting and happy marriages. Adult experiencers, on the other hand, had tremendous difficulty forming or maintaining stable relationships afterward; 78 percent of their marriages ended in divorce.

Both groups in my study reported unusual increases or decreases in light sensitivity: about 75 percent with kids; close to the adult range of 80 to 90 percent. Seventy-three percent of the adults went on to experience electrical sensitivity, but not many children did – only 52 percent. This may reflect adults' access to technological equipment rather than a true deviation. Older experiencers are four times more likely to become vegetarians than the younger crowd – even near-death kids snub their veggies.

Parent-sibling relationships tend to be strained for child experiencers. Additionally, kids are more likely than adults to suffer socially and to report having regrets about what happened to them. An astounding number of children would go back to the "Other Side of Death's Curtain" after their experience, even if that meant suicide. Child experiencers, whether still young or grown, seldom see a counselor, and receive less help if they do. This is not true with adult experiencers – contrary to how loudly they may protest. Because the disparity between children and adults in this area is so enormous, it begs further comment.

Angel leading a child to the Other Side. Credit: Getty Images.

One-third of the child experiencers in my study admitted to having serious problems with alcohol within five to 10 years after their experience. Almost to a person, they claimed that undeveloped social and communication skills were the culprits, along with an inability to understand what motivated the people around them. Their world view, as it turned out, had altered significantly from their peer group and family members, making it difficult for them to "fit back in."

There's another aspect to the issue of alienation that, for the child, may be even more profound. Completely aside from any abuse or peer pressure from family or friends, and whether or not parents are supportive, the major factor in a child's experience appears to be who or what greeted the youngster on The Other Side of death. What parent, no matter how wonderful or loving, can compare with the Holy Spirit? What person, friend or foe, can interest a child who has visited the bright realms and become buddies with an angel? Connecting with such transcendent love, and then abruptly losing that connection, can be very confusing, even devastating. Many kids expressed guilt-ridden laments like: "I'm really bad. The bright ones left, and I can't find them anymore. It's all my fault they're gone."

We tend to forget how personally children take everything, and the extent to which they blame themselves if things go awry. Nor do we notice how large things loom for them – their near-death experience can define their entire world. Because many are unable to make "before and after" comparisons, the fact that "here" is not the same as "there" is often too foreign a concept for them to grasp.

Suicide

Children reason differently. Unaccustomed to considering cause and effect, they tend to act on impulse; hence the high degree of alcoholism, and an attempted suicide rate of 21 percent. It seems perfectly logical to a child that the way to rejoin the light beings met in death is simply to die and go back.

This is not recognized by them as self-destructive. Their logic says: "I was in this beautiful place while I wasn't breathing. It all went away when my breath came back. I need to stop my breath so I can return."

Parent/child bonding is initially quite strong. These kids want to be with their families. That bonding brings them back again and again. Common assertions are: "I came back to help my daddy"; or "I came back so Mommy won't cry." The parent/child bond doesn't begin to stretch thin or break until after the child revives. That climate of welcome or threat they are greeted with directly impinges on everything that comes next.

To understand children's cases, we must keep in mind that kids are tuned to different harmonics than adults. Concepts of life and death leave them with puzzled faces. "I don't end or begin anywhere," a youngster once told me. "I just reach out and catch the next wave that goes by and hop a ride. That's how I got here."

This child, like other young experiencers, speaks in the language of "other worlds," one that is less verbal and more akin to synesthesia-multiple sensing. This enables them to perceive "reality" as a series of layered realms, unhampered by physical boundaries. They easily giggle with angels, play with ghosts, and pre-experience the future. Parents generally find such behavior cause for panic. Yet what seems worrisome may have a simple explanation: near-death states expand and enhance faculties normal to us, allowing access to more of the electromagnetic spectrum – the typical range of human perception is a mere one percent.

Growth in intelligence

As a child's mind begins to shift from what happened to them, their intelligence quotient rises. Here are a few sample percentages from my book, *Children of the New Millennium* (1999), which details my research with child experiencers:

- Mind works differently – highly creative and inventive: 84 percent.
- Significant enhancement of intellect: 68 percent.
- Mind tested at genius level (overall/from birth to age 15): 48 percent.
- Mind tested at genius level (subgroup, those under age 6): 81 percent.
- Drawn to and highly proficient in math, science or history: 93 percent.

After a near-death experience, a child's learning ability reverses. Instead of continuing with the typical developmental curve – from concrete details to abstract concepts – a child returns immersed in broad conceptual reasoning styles and has to learn how to go from abstract back to concrete. One first-grader returned to school after drowning and being resuscitated. While his peers continued with their reading of "See Spot Run," he wanted to know about Greek mythology and why Robinson Crusoe was written. His teacher was stunned, but he just blinked his eyes and headed for the library.

The most oft-repeated phrase from those I interviewed was: "I felt like an adult in a child's body."

Even those who did not test out with extraordinarily high IQs (which averaged around 150 to 160; several were 184 and above) evidenced uniquely creative and intuitive minds, numerous faculty enhancements, an unrelenting curiosity and exceptional knowledge soon after reviving. Some were gifted with foreign languages. Adult experiencers also returned more intelligent than before, and many became intuitive problem solvers. All of this occurred without genetic markers of any kind to account for what happened.

Overall, child experiencers are natural computer whizzes. Many become physicists and inventors once grown, or masters of the arts and humanities; some are professional psychics. Older teenage and adult experiencers are most often drawn to healing, counseling and ministerial roles afterward. Not so the kids – at least not the majority. But mention math or science and they're all aglow. History intrigues them, along with anything to do with times past, as if it might apply to who they were before in past lives.

Most (85 percent) of the kids with the greatest acceleration in mathematical ability also acquired an intense and passionate love of music. In the brain, math and music functions are located next to each other. Children's near-death states seem to activate both regions, as if they were a single unit.

The child who returns from a near-death episode is a remodeled, rewired and refined version of the original. The changes children undergo are more dramatic than those of adults – not, I suspect, because their aftereffects are different, but because they are still in the process of basic brain development when the episode occurs. They are hit with a life-changing experience at a time when they are most vulnerable to the power of such a shift.

How many children are affected? Thanks to a poll taken in 1997 by *US News & World Report,* the estimate for near-death experiencers in the United States has jumped to 15 million people. That translates to about one-third of those who brush death, nearly die or who are pronounced clinically dead but later revive. However, this estimate only addresses adults.

Melvin Morse, MD, in his pioneering book, *Closer to the Light* (1990), puts the figure at around 70 percent for children. Thus, under the same circumstances, children are twice as likely as adults to experience a near-death episode.

Modern resuscitation techniques and new medical technologies are bringing back from the edge of death more and more people – especially kids – who return ideally suited for this high-tech world. It's as if the very citizens we need to thrive in our new global village are being created right under our noses.

Millennial generation
Even more amazing is that the Millennial Generation is being born this way. Today's crop of kids compares almost trait-for-trait with what happens to children after a near-death experience.

In *Generations: The History of America's Future, 1584 to 2069* (1991), historians William Strauss and Neil Howe identify the Millennial Generation as the group of children born between 1982 and about 2003. These young people comprise the fourteenth generation since the United States became a nation. They are the most wanted, nurtured and educated group of individuals we've ever produced, and the most protected by law. Unusually smart and assertive, they are as creative and intuitive as they are technologically adept. They score higher on IQ tests than any other generation on record – a 24- to 26-point hike; a significant percentage of them test between 150 to 160 or higher. But they receive their greatest scores in non-verbal intelligence. They are creative problem solvers and intuitive innovators. This jump is so high that changes in the gene pool cannot possibly account for it. Neither can education, as test scores in the area of rote schooling rose only slightly – a puzzle for educators.

Something of note is happening to the human family – these anomalies are global – and it is happening now!

Increasing numbers of children are born "advanced." Increasing numbers of children are becoming "advanced." Increasing numbers of adults, through near-death states or because of an intense transformation of consciousness, are also becoming "advanced."

Brain shifts
Because this is true, I no longer consider near-death states a separate phenomenon, but part of the larger category of consciousness transformations. I call such episodes "brain shifts" because they appear to cause a structural, chemical and functional change in the experiencer's brain, not to mention alterations in his or her nervous and digestive systems, attitudes, and sense of self.

Brain shifts can result from any manner of otherworldly occurrences. Some are turbulent: religious conversions, near-death episodes, kundalini breakthroughs, shamanistic rituals, sudden spiritual transformations, certain types of head trauma, and being struck by lightning. Some brain shifts are tranquil: the slow, steady application of spiritual disciplines, mindfulness techniques, meditation, vision quests, or the results of a prayerful state of mind in which the individual simply desires to become a better person.

Major characteristics displayed by people who have undergone or who are going through a brain shift include physiological changes in thought-processing (a switch from sequential or selective thinking to clustered thinking and an acceptance of ambiguity), insatiable curiosity, heightened intelligence, more creativity and invention, unusual sensitivity to light and sound, substantially more or less energy (even energy surges and oftentimes more sexual), reversal of the body clock, lower blood pressure, accelerated metabolic and substance absorption rates (decreased tolerance of pharmaceuticals and chemically-treated products), electrical sensitivity, synesthesia (multiple sensing), increased allergies or sensitivities, a new preference for vegetables and grains (and less meat for adults), and even changes toward a more youthful appearance – before and after photographs can differ significantly.

Psychological changes include losing the fear of death, greater spirituality (and less "religiosity"), greater abilities in abstract and philosophical thinking, bouts of depression, disregard for time, greater generosity and charity, expansive concepts of love (while at the same time they are challenged to initiate and maintain satisfying relationships), exaggerated inner child issues, lower competitive attitudes, greater conviction of a life purpose, rejection of previous limitations and norms, increased psychic ability and future memory episodes (pre-living the future), charisma, childlike sense of joy and wonder if adult, greater maturity if a child, detachment and dissociation, and a hunger for knowledge and learning.

The Greater Plan

In reconsidering near-death states, I now regard adult episodes as a growth event, an opportunity for the experiencer to make course corrections in his or her life; a second chance. I see childhood episodes as evolutionary events – part of a quantum leap in life development and growth of humankind as a species; a second birth. The larger category – transformations of consciousness – I have come to recognize as the engine that drives evolution, and which advances us.

Beyond all stories and revelations experiencers share (and some are quite spectacular), is "a larger presence and a greater plan." My three near-death experiences, occurring in the first three months of 1977, opened the door to this vision. The thousands of people I have interviewed and studied since then reflect the same awakening: We are co-creators with our Creator, advancing with Creation itself.

Most repeated from near-death experiencers are these four words: "Always there is life." If they are right, and I believe they are, then how can there be an afterlife? A before-life? A death?

Kids describe life as "the stream we flow along," while negotiating the currents and eddies of its spread. It is the "homey home" of our visions and the ever-present reality of each moment. Life is all there is. Children are really quite wise, and we would be wise to listen to them.

PMH Atwater: Internationally renowned NDE researcher and author.

FATE June 2000

VISIONARY BUSINESS
Frank Spaeth

"Without being aware of it," Marc Allen recalls, "I had this fear of death and this real fear of eternity and what was beyond death. I remember as a kid, 12 to 13 years old, lying awake nights fearing death and what was beyond, almost to the point of panic."

Marc grew up in Minnesota, and he graduated from the University of Minnesota in 1968 with a degree in theater. Then he joined the Firehouse Theater in Minneapolis, where his work nearly cost him his life.

"We were doing this wild adaptation of the play *Faust*, about Western man and his search for knowledge," Marc recalls. "We all played Faust at different times. I played him as a lover, which was great, but then I also played him as the scientist that society persecutes, like Galileo. They put me up in this tower that had three ropes hanging from it, and they would throw me off the tower. I had a rope around my neck and one around my arm and another around my leg."

Marc was supposed to catch himself with his arm and leg and hang from the rope. Unfortunately, during one performance something went wrong.

Clinging to life

"I actually hung. I was actually dying. My experience was euphoric. Incredibly euphoric. One of the happiest, most vitally alive, euphoric moments of my life. I was suddenly soaring over these hills, beautiful hill dotted with oak trees. I still don't know whether it was in Northern California or somewhere else, because I found out later that some of the countryside looks like that – Marin County and the foothills of the mountains – or if I was in some other dimension. I don't know. But I was completely out of my body. I remember looking around for my body and I couldn't see it, but it didn't matter. It was wonderful.

"I flew at great speeds and then I hit a turbulence, like the kind you hit in a plane. The ride got bumpy. Then I found myself (and this was way before *Embraced by the Light*) looking around in a circle, and I remember thinking, because I was so totally conscious, 'Gee, if I had a body now I'd be sick to my stomach,' because I was going around a circle that was getting nauseating. I looked around and I was in this big funnel, on the inside, going around and around, and there was light at the top.

"I felt I had a choice. I had a choice whether to go on into the next life, and that was very exciting and wonderful, or whether to come back to this life. I got a feeling that there was some reason I was supposed to go back. I was not finished with this life. The lessons had not been learned. But I really didn't want to come back. It felt like going back to kindergarten when I had been in graduate school or beyond. But I went back and I kind of willed myself up to the top of this cone and broke through the light and right back into my body.

"I had regained consciousness and I was staring into the face of the director, who saw that I was dying. He ran and got a ladder and lifted me up out of the ropes, and that's when I came back. That experience changed my life."

Marc decided that it was "time to grow up and do what I was supposed to be doing, and that was instrumental in leaving the theater and studying Zen, and it changed my fear of death. I realized that beyond death is an exciting transformation and a new life that I look forward to. When this life's complete, I'm ready for the next one."

Marc studied Zen and meditation for two years, including five-and-a-half months on Maui. He then spent three-and-a-half years studying Tibetan Buddhism, which he would not recommend to any Westerner. "It is very hard to adapt Tibetan Buddhism to Western culture. The two cultures are so diverse, and it is such a complex thing. Zen, however, is very easy to adapt to America. In a way, the Japanese are very Western, especially with their workaholic attitudes."

In 1974, Marc began his journey toward the business world. He began teaching meditation seminars with a woman named Shakti Gawain. As Marc describes it, the two got tricked into doing workshops.

The workshops were a big success, and after one event Marc decided that he wanted everybody to have something to take home. He wrote four pages of notes, photocopied them, and handed them out to his next group. After each session he added more notes until he had a 64-page book. "I started having to charge a few dollars to cover the printing cost," Marc recalls. This was how he stumbled into the writing and publishing businesses. "I never intended to write a book. I never intended to start a publishing company. But one thing led to another and both things happened."

A powerful dream

Early in the formation of his business, Marc had a dream:

> *It was the most powerful dream I ever had. I was this mess of conflicting core beliefs, and my business was a struggle because of it. Part of me was not even sure about making money. I was worried that I might become greedy and forget the higher spiritual things in life. I was also doing Western magick at the time and I had conflicting beliefs about that.*
>
> *Then one night I had this dream. I was climbing this mountain. It was really rocky and difficult. Suddenly, a path opened to the right of me that was very easy. I started walking up the path and I saw this gate that went into the mountain. It had a big, wrought-iron lock on it. I went up to the lock and realized that it was a puzzle. I pulled a key out of the lock and it was a sword. It fit my*

hand perfectly, and the door swung open. I entered this scary, dark cave, but I had my sword with me. The cave got smaller and darker and scarier, but then I saw a little golden light. I went through this little door and it opened into a huge, vaulted cathedral.

There were three banquet tables in the center of this cathedral. I walked up to the first one and it was loaded with money and gold and houses and sport cars, just loaded. This voice, this wordless voice, said very clearly, "This is the material plane. There is nothing to reject in this, so master it and enjoy it."

Then I went to the second table, and it had the five symbols of the Tarot. The voice said, "This is the astral plane, the plane of magic. There is nothing here to reject, so master it and enjoy it."

Then I went to the final table. It was shimmering and clothed in fine white cloth. It had nothing on it. And the voice said, "This is the spiritual plane. You've always been here and you'll always be here. Enjoy your life."

I laid back and I floated up to the center of the cathedral, and I felt this golden light shower through me. Then I woke up in bed with my arms out, still feeling the light.

That dream changed my life. I realized that I had all these negative core beliefs about money and they were just that – negative. Money can do a lot of good in the world. In fact, it's essential to do a lot of good in the world.

One of the keys in Marc's book, *Visionary Business*, deals with reflecting on life's past events and discovering the core beliefs those events have created. He feels that core beliefs not only affect a person's life, but also one's business.

"Every business reflects the consciousness of its owner. That consciousness is the total sum of all the things that go through our head, and all the deep core beliefs we've picked up since childhood about how the world works. The fascinating thing about these beliefs to me is that we've all got a ton of them and they're contradictory," he says.

Marc stresses the contradiction between the positive core beliefs within each of us and the negative cultural core beliefs brought on by events like the Great Depression.

"When something bad happens, we have to look at our own beliefs and see if we can find any opportunity in the adversity. The people who can see the opportunities in adversity are the ones who become successful," he says. Marc feels that when negative core beliefs outweigh the positive ones, people destine themselves to failure. By overcoming negative beliefs, people bring success to themselves.

Another key to becoming successful is to visualize success, he says. "It is essential to envision our success very clearly, and that's what visualization is. It is a step that a lot of people miss." Marc says people have to decide what they want to do and then do it.

The next step is to visualize being successful at it. "We can never create success without first imagining it. No one has ever gotten a paycheck without first visualizing it. They go to work for it and then they get it. Or, you never have lunch without visualizing it. There is nothing new about visualization. We do it every minute of every day. Before you can succeed, you have to first visualize your success."

The spiritual side of business

Marc strongly believes that there is a spiritual side to business. He states, "Every moment of life has a spiritual side. Just as there is a physical, mental and emotional side to business, so there is also a spiritual side. Creating anything is mystical. The essence of creation can only be explained mystically or spiritually. How do we create anything? It is all very mysterious."

Marc has found his study of Western magic very useful in business. "I have an exercise in the book that I do. I take a white piece of paper and draw a five-pointed star on it. At the top point I write 'God's will.' For those who don't believe in God, they can put whatever they relate to for strength. Then, at each of the other points, I put my four main goals, and I meditate on them every day. I keep the visualization in my mind, and before I know it, the thing manifests. That's mystical! For me to go from having no income, to $800 income, to working up to $15 million income—to me it's a mystery. It's magical."

Marc Allen's book, *Visionary Business*, goes far beyond business. It speaks of improving every individual and every aspect of the world.

Twelve keys to visionary business

"Visionary business" means envisioning success for one's endeavor while at the same time benefiting employees, the community, and society as a whole. Marc Allen's book lists 12 keys to running a business in a successful, visionary way.

1) Imagine your ideal scene.

2) Write your business plan as a clear and concrete visualization.

3) Discover your higher purpose.

4) See the benefits within adversity and keep picturing success.

5) Plan your work and work your plan: the employee handbook, benefits, profit sharing and stock options.

6) Avoid management by crisis: make a clear annual goal.

7) Give abundantly and reap the rewards.

8) "Love chance, learn to dance, and leave J. Edgar Hoover behind." (In other words, learn to accept change, learn to satisfy the customer and learn to trust your employees.)

9) Reflect on the events that have shaped your life and discover the core beliefs you have created for yourself because of those events.

10) Evolve through the three stages of a business: infancy, adolescence, adulthood.

11) Consider the mystical and spiritual side of business: Practice your own effective magic.

12) Do what you love to do, and you'll create a visionary business in your own absolutely unique way.

FATE June 1996

AN UNCONVENTIONAL NEAR-DEATH EXPERIENCE
Bruce Pont

I have had two near-death experiences in which my consciousness separated from my body. One of the experiences – the second – was quite profound and different from the "model" that is discussed so much in the literature and media.

My first experience happened in 2009. I was a regular guy, extremely fit and involved in sports. I was a businessman, a company director, and I traveled around the world. I was married and had five kids. I had never been into drugs and only occasionally consumed alcohol. I was a longtime practitioner of meditation and meditative practices including Transcendental Meditation® and TM® Siddhis, the Monroe Institute, martial arts and more than 50 fire-walks. I didn't think much about death and what the afterlife is like.

I went to the hospital for some surgery. The anesthesiologist gave me a spinal anesthetic, something I had never had before. I'd had general anesthesia before without a problem. I have a low heart rate and it's in the medical literature that a "spinal" on a person with a low heart rate can lead to an SCA, i.e., sudden cardiac arrest, which is what happened to me.

After the surgery was completed, I went into cardiac arrest after I was taken to a private room. My wife, who is an intensive care nurse in the same hospital, was with me. My heart rate was fading fast. I just had time enough to say, "Girls, I'm not feeling very well," and it was lights out, literally lights out. I was a "code blue." I don't remember any of it. They jumped on my chest and put some drugs, including atropine, into me to try to get my heart started again.

It happened just after 2 PM in the afternoon. I was unconscious for a period of some 20 minutes. I was clinically dead for a while but wherever I was, I was still alive. I didn't know where I was, what I was or who I was. My consciousness had separated from the rest of me and my human body was left there along with my mind in whatever form there was in the chemical biological sense. To me, mind functions entirely separately and distinctly different from consciousness, but the two work together synergistically. My consciousness was trying to make sense of a significant separation from my mind and body.

I didn't go through any mysterious tunnels. There came a point in the 20 minutes – and I don't know precisely where that point was – where my consciousness started to merge back into my mind and body. I appeared to be traveling through an inverted cone, shaped like a waffle cone, coming from the small end and going toward the big end. It was etheric in nature and had a grayish white texture and appearance and within it. "I" was and "it" was swirling and pulsating.

A lot of yellow shapes and figures and weird faces then appeared around me, which I couldn't understand. Eventually I recognized the top of the ceiling and a physical light of my hospital room. I saw human shapes lined up against the wall, which I found out later were the resuscitation and medical team standing at the foot of my bed. After a time, my cognitive function improved to the point where I could understand where I was.

My return was very similar to the words that Dr. Eben Alexander later used to talk about his NDE. I read his book [*Proof of Heaven*, 2012] in March of 2013. At the time of my experience I had no knowledge of his book or his words. His description of coming back to life again was almost identical to what I had experienced several years earlier.

My second and more profound NDE happened in August 2012, when I was 62. I'd gone to the hospital for a routine colonoscopy under general anesthesia in the morning; the staff had taken great precautions because of my earlier experience.

Afterwards my wife brought me back home. I was resting in bed when suddenly I started to fade. My heart rate and blood pressure dropped. I went into what is called "vasovagal syncope," a sign of impending collapse. Vasovagals are triggered by drops in heart rate and blood pressure; a vagus nerve response. It is a well-known condition and many people have it but my particular neurocardiogenic-dysautonomia condition is extremely rare and considerably more life-threatening. I never had the condition prior to my spinal anesthetic-induced cardiac arrest and now I live with it every day.

My heart rate and blood pressure then plummeted. I was fast approaching cardiac flatline. My wife called the paramedics. Two senior paramedics arrived and said that they had not seen anything like my condition. My wife told them to inject me immediately with atropine, a potent cardiac stimulant – but too much and it's a poison. The paramedics had to get permission from the hospital chief medical officer to inject it.

They started me off conservatively at 250 mcg IV – the maximum dosage authorized was 1200 mcg. I was conscious in that I could hear and understand what was happening. But I was heading down. They put another 250 in and another 250 and then quickly took me up to the 1200 mcg maximum, and then took me off to the hospital.

They took me to an emergency room bed, which, I later learned, was the same bed that my late mother was in when she had a cardiac arrest and nearly died. That was a bit freaky.

I was given another intravenous drug called glycopyrrolate, which can be administered for adverse reactions with surgeries and also for other conditions; in my case to block the parasympathetic nerve reflexes that were driving my heart rate and blood pressure down. My heart rate and blood pressure were still dropping, but not as fast. There was nothing more they could do. It was wait and see, wait and see. Many hours passed.

By then it was late at night. My wife and young daughter stayed with me in my room. My NDE started around 3 o'clock in the morning. Everything was quiet. My ICU wife was in a chair on my left side, watching my vitals on the monitor, ready to press the emergency button if I arrested. My daughter was asleep in a chair on my right side. I was lying with my head inclined and my feet up to try to get some blood to my head.

Suddenly I left my body. I was gone. I found myself in a place that I'd been to before. It was what I call The Void – the black Void that was familiar to me in deep meditation. There was nothing in the black Void initially except me. I was both the observer and the observed. I was looking at myself as I was looking at me looking at myself, if that makes sense. Then those two perceptions merged so that I was looking at only what was ahead of me in my environment.

A portal appeared in front of me. It was rectangular with defined sides but not solid. It was about the size of a double garage door, but a bit higher. It was etheric in nature, a light white grayish color, like smoke.

I knew intuitively where I was, and that this was The Transition. I moved toward the portal, and I could see coming from the other side *beings* moving toward me. I knew this was the crossover point for me between physical life and physical death, and that if I went through that rectangle there would be no coming back – there would be no life for me in human form. I knew absolutely that there would be no reentry to physical life.

This absolute knowing permeated me. I was comfortable, relaxed and not scared. Apprehensive, maybe, to a small degree. I moved toward the portal but had no intention of crossing. I just felt I had to go there, to the edge, because I knew there was more to this even though I couldn't see far beyond the portal itself.

As I did so, the beings kept moving toward me. They were walking slowly in a formation like the tip of an arrow. There was one in the center at the point, one at each side, and two at the back. The one at the front was clearly the leader. Behind these five were a couple more beings in the background, which I wasn't taking much notice of.

They all looked identical in human shape and size. They were slim and about 1.8 metres tall [about six feet]. They were translucent and were covered with shimmering, translucent shrouds. The shrouds had a very light, brown-gold cast to them – I can't describe it in human words. There was immense light coming from within the shrouds.

The five in formation came forward simultaneously, and simultaneously they put out their hands as a welcome. I had the impression they had their palms turned up, but their hands were covered by their shrouds. Their faces were covered as well. There were no features other than a general shape of a human. I knew that they did not want me to see any more of them because they were not human; they were light!

We all stopped at the boundary of the portal, me on one side and the beings on the other. I wasn't scared. I knew what all this was about. We communicated telepathically. They invited me to come on over. I felt entirely comfortable with that. If my circumstances had been different I would have crossed over and gone home. But I had ties and obligations to my wife and family, things I needed to finish.

I thanked them for the invitation. I explained my situation, and asked, "Do I really have to go? I don't want to." The beings replied that this time my crossing was not mandatory. I was grateful and expressed thanks for the opportunity. That was the end of the light show.

I literally snapped back into my body like I was on the end of a huge rubber band stretched out and released from outer space. I hit my body with such force that I felt myself bounce in bed and my upper body jerk upwards. I announced to myself, "I'm back!" I looked around slowly. I saw my daughter, who was still asleep. My wife was awake and had been watching my vital signs on the monitor. She said, "Welcome back. Where have you been?" Whilst stroking my forehead she gently said, "You are OK now, just relax and sleep."

My vital signs came back to normal and I was discharged from hospital that very morning. Interestingly, during my NDE my wife said that my vital signs did not fluctuate or change at all. This is yet further evidence to me that consciousness is an independent "entity" unaffected by the human biology. How it integrates with the human mind and biological body is the true mystery of life.

This was real, not a dream, not a hallucination and not caused by the cardiac drugs. The drugs had worn off many hours before, anyway, due to their very short half-life spans (atropine <2 hours, glycopyrrolate <1 hour).

It was the most profound experience that has ever happened in my life. Consciousness, the spiritual, everything just merged. The most important thing about it, beyond not crossing, was that I understood that when my death comes, this is my destiny. Home is on the other side of that dividing line. I also understand that the dividing line may be different for each person, presented in a personally meaningful way.

Like others who have had NDEs, I came back significantly changed. My advice to others is to be grateful for your life and what you have. Gratitude is the single most important word in a person's vocabulary. You must *feel* it. I'm grateful to be given the opportunity to come back and spend time with my family. I take comfort in knowing there is considerably more than what we see and hear in the physical world. Death is not the death of us, just the end of the physical vehicle.

My NDE did not make me more "religious" in any sense – I think that religions are about controlling people. I am a deeply spiritual person, and always have been. My place on the planet has been one of provider and stability as a patriarch of a family. I have accomplished that. My greatest yearning is my spiritual journey of learning. Meditation is important to me. It opens channels in your consciousness, and the more your channels are open, the more opportunities are presented to you.

I am not frightened of death, but I don't seek to accelerate its arrival. However, I know that when my time comes, and I don't have the opportunity to step back from it, what is on the other side of that portal is a great place to go.

I have shared my very personal and intimate NDE experience with several terminally ill family members before they each passed over, including my late Mum. They were very comforted and said that they were no longer scared of what was coming. I have only told a limited number of other special friends; their responses have been overwhelming, encouraging me to share my story for all. This is why I am now sharing this publicly and I hope that it may be of benefit to you, too.

My heartfelt thanks to Rosemary for publishing my story.
Namaste ~ Bruce (2018) Australia

[Note: I met Bruce Pont at a conference in Byron Bay, Australia in 2017, where he shared these experiences with me, and generously agreed to have them published to a wider audience. –REG]

THE GIRL WHO DIED ... AGAIN
Michael T. Shoemaker

A long-forgotten incident shows that a hysteria-induced coma can resemble a near-death experience. The case could well be called a "spontaneous NDE" and demonstrates that such phenomena are by no means recent. It was described in the *Albany* [N.Y.] *Evening Journal* on December 21, 1867.

A 17-year-old servant girl named Van Arsdale lived with her employers in Whiteland, Indiana. When she had "taken sick with something like hysteria" the family confined her to bed for more than a week, and then the girl seemed to die. But physicians detected a faint pulse and prevented her burial.

After 12 hours in deep coma, Miss Van Arsdale returned to normal and astonished everyone by saying "she had visited heaven and hell and had conversed with the Savior and many persons whom she had known on earth…" To prove her statements, she "sent for a number of persons in the neighborhood and not only imparted to them news of (deceased) friends but told of sins committed by them, (supposedly) unknown by anyone…"

Then Miss Van Arsdale announced she would have a second trance. Again, her pulse and respiration nearly stopped. A physician pricked her body to see if she was faking but was "perfectly convinced" that she was not.

On reviving, she "seemed unable to describe the places she had been in but gave histories of events and persons with remarkable minuteness… Finally, she added, oddly, that 'she would never have a recurrence of the trance unless she should commit some flagrant sin.'"

Regarded as especially amazing was "her sending for persons to whom, before her illness, she would have been afraid to (speak)… and telling them stories and facts not the most palatable to such worldly people."

The *Journal* article concluded with assurances that many "eminently respectable" citizens attested to the facts of Miss Van Arsdale's deathlike trances.

FATE November 1984

BEYOND THE ETHERIC VEIL
Ernest Groth

The most intriguing question of all time concerns life in the world after death – if there is such a world.

John Puckering was dead of heart failure. His body lay on an operating table in a London hospital. Dr. G. Percivel Mills massaged the heart "only from a sense of duty, and without real hope of success." Then came a faint pulse. Artificial respiration was applied, and after anxious minutes, John Puckering returned to consciousness. He was discharged as cured, and it was so reported by the *British Medical Journal*.

But John Puckering was not happy about his return to life. In 1935 he made a statement to newspaper reporters: "I wish Dr. Mills had not brought me back… I found myself in a room, much bigger than any room I have ever seen. It must have been night, for the room was lighted very clearly. The light was brighter than electric light, yet somehow comforting… I did not notice any lamps. I did not notice any of the surroundings, because I was so interested in the people in the room. There were a lot of them… All grown up men and women. They wore clothes like you and I and looked like ordinary people. They were like very healthy people who are out of doors most of the time.

"I felt awkward. I wondered what to do. But that soon passed off, because all the people looked so friendly. They smiled at me. Everybody there looked so happy. I saw my wife. She died, as people say, more than a year ago, but I saw her there clearly and she looked very happy. "I saw other people I used to know. There was one man who used to be the postman. He died five years ago. And there was another who passed away seven years ago. When I looked at him, he knew who I was. He smiled at me and nodded. Then somehow the light in the room began to change. It was as though daylight was coming. I don't remember any more."

For John Puckering, death had lost its fearful qualities, and he told everyone so. Medical authority states he was dead, and it states that he was revived from death. It is one of the best cases on record which give us a glimpse into the world after death. It is a fact that John Puckering died... and lived again!

FATE Spring 1948

VISIONARY EXPERIENCES AND TRANSFORMATION

SPIRITUAL, MYSTICAL AND EXTRAORDINARY EXPERIENCES: LIFE-CHANGING TRANSFORMATIONS
Bob Davis, PhD

Introduction

The great divide between the physical world and that of the mind or spirit did not prevent great scientists like Galileo, Copernicus, Einstein, Kepler and Newton from having a deep spiritual mindset, as their writings affirm. And today, there is a resurgence of spirituality with more and more people having personal spiritual, mystical and extraordinary experiences (SMEE).

A SMEE represents types of altered states of consciousness and associated encounters with a supernatural world. SMEEs, which appear to incorporate indescribable awareness of time, space and physical reality, often characterized by perceptions of oneness/interconnectedness with the universe, positive emotions, alterations of time and/or space, feeling one's consciousness separating from the body, telepathic communication, and insight and wisdom, have been widely reported across cultures and throughout human history. Survey research, for instance, has reported that about one-third of Americans have had intense spiritual experiences, and that about 10-15 percent of the general population has had an out-of-body experience (OBE) and/or near-death experience (NDE), with an estimated 200,000 people in the United States and millions worldwide reporting a NDE every year.

    The high incidence of reported SMEEs alone eludes my ability to adequately explain. Even more astonishing is the remarkable similarity of detailed accounts of SMEEs reported by those who contend to have had no communication with those who had the same experience. Such accounts apply not only to the similarity of the experience but also to the details of reported increases in intuitive and psychic capabilities, and changes in attitudes about health, life, and spirituality, among other psycho-spiritual transformations.

Self-transcendence
A SMEE can have generally positive transformative aftereffects, with some subjects reporting them to be among the most important experiences in their lives; a self-transcendent experience that can be life changing. As part of a SMEE, for example, one may suddenly experience the world as a manifestation of one cosmic creative energy; nothing is separate. Features may include visions or communications with deceased loved ones, religious figures, God, the light, angels, beings of light or other nonphysical beings. The realization of this unseen reality facilitates an awareness which provides a new perspective on life by which everyday reality is viewed differently and becomes a focal point of change in the person's life. These realms are not opinion but fact to those who have experienced them.

    The SMEE, and its associated behavioral outcomes and realized new knowledge, influences the individual to turn attention away from the "self" toward a feeling of being more connected to humanity that touches their lives in a pronounced way. They speak of a newfound, awe-inspiring connection to humanity, life and God, Source or Creator. The experience and the knowledge, and its impact on that person's life, are at the very center of that person's being. This is what individuals report as represented in common statements such as, "I just communed with the universal knowing and being, as if I were the universe… I mean, the conviction was absolute: I know everything that is in the universe. There's nothing that I don't know. And I know it. And I was it." In fact, a friend of mine who had a SMEE triggered from a NDE wrote: "My near-death experiences definitively convinced me that consciousness is not held in the brain, like some sort of component, but rather, is accessible via the brain. My work as a nurse further solidified my belief that consciousness is indeed non-local. As patients neared death, it was clear to me they were communicating with and accessing other realms." And for some reason, the experience seems to eventually transform them in terms of their personal and philosophical viewpoints.

A transformative SMEE occurs when people perceive themselves and the world profoundly differently. Altered personal and philosophical values, priorities and appreciation of the purpose of life can be catalysts for spiritual transformation. During SMEEs, people can feel a sense of connection with other individuals, humankind, and even existence itself. Some experiences are sought after and triggered through meditation, yoga, drugs, religious practices and sensory deprivation or prayer. Other experiences can happen spontaneously, as with OBEs and NDEs, personal trauma and illness. Many of these experiences contain messages, guidance, premonitions, or reviews of one's life.

The integration process resulting from a SMEE may evolve over many years as the individual reflects upon the meaning and values drawn from the experience, which can bring difficult challenges. This process and the associated desired outcomes are highly individualized. There is no one size fits all. But once the experience and its accompanying challenges have been fully integrated, the following attributes may become part of the person's life: Changes in values, a greater sense of well-being, a more positive outlook on life, a greater desire to learn, increased creativity and psychic abilities, greater empathy, compassion, and sense of purpose, loss of the fear of death, and improved behavior and attitude toward others. Many also experience unconditional love, and a greater acceptance and tolerance of people of different religious faiths than before.

A SMEE may result in one finding less value in impressing others or adhering to hierarchies or routines. More importance may be placed on family, health, and the environment and spirituality, rather than focusing on money or fame. Destruction of the environment may be especially painful and a cause for activism. Emphasis is also placed on positively influencing people with deeper, more spiritual values. A SMEE can also alter some or all of an individual's prior held spiritual or religious beliefs. Atheists may report complete conversions to spirituality or religion. Some report leaving their religious communities for a more spiritual, individual approach to life and spirit. Some find confirmation and strengthening of their pre-existing spiritual or religious beliefs in their experiences. Some may begin a journey of seeking out a faith that is consistent with their experience. Experiencers may devote increasing amounts of time and energy into families, caring for children, animals, the sick or dying, or volunteering for nonprofit causes.

Challenges

One of the greatest challenges for those who have a SMEE is the impact of their experience on family members. It is not uncommon for significant others to strive to understand their loved one's experience, question its validity, and be confused by the "stranger" their loved one has become. For those who have a NDE, for example, separation is common and approximately 75 percent divorce within 7-10 years. Psychiatrist Dr. Bruce Greyson, who reviewed the literature over the past 30 years on the behavioral effects of NDEs, concluded that this type of SMEE typically produces "positive changes in attitudes, beliefs, and values, but may also lead to interpersonal and intrapsychic problems." Spouses commonly report they no longer know or understand their loved one. The most common complaint from spouses was: "I don't know this person anymore." A common attitude of the experiencer was, "Since I no longer fit in, I'll move on." The general mindset was that significant others were convinced that the experiencer was out-of-touch with reality, while the experiencer became convinced that significant others were not interested in making changes.

It is also very common for those who have had a SMEE to report an enhanced sensitivity to strong emotions and negative behaviors. Typical comments are: "I had to be alone with my senses a lot"; "this caused a problem with my relationships"; "it's hard for other people to understand why I am so sensitive"; "I feel other people's pain"; "I would pick up on people's anxiety and get stomach problems"; and "I walk out of places that feel evil." Quite interestingly, some even contend being told they have a purpose, that everything happens for a reason, and that we choose our lessons. Comments may include: "It's all homework"; "it's not the experience, but how we respond to it"; and "in order to appreciate life more, we must experience loss."

Perhaps the most common takeaway from those reporting a SMEE is the importance of unconditional love and how we treat each other on earth. According to my colleague, a SMEE "can bring friction in almost all important areas of an experiencer's life. The experience affects relationships with others, careers, money, religion, spirituality, etc. After an out-of-body experience, many people report an inner awakening of their spiritual identity, a transformation of their self-concept. They see themselves as more than matter – more aware and alive. They express a profound inner wisdom based on personal spiritual experience. Many report being connected to something greater than themselves, connected to the very source of life. They report a powerful feeling of breaking through a dense barrier of ignorance, fear, and limitation."

Related to this remarkable transformative experience is the research by an authority and pioneer on near-death states, PMH Atwater. Her work established that the SMEE induced by a near-death state is part of the larger genre of transformations of consciousness. This notion may be depicted in selected excerpts from her extensive collection of fascinating psychological aftereffects in nearly 7,000 people, as follows:

> "All I was taught in my life became irrelevant. I was transformed. I was forced to grow and that has made me a better person, still not with all the answers, but inquisitive about the unknown."

> "Because of these experiences, I am a much more open-minded person. I have such a broader perspective on life."

> "Happier, more open-minded, a belief in the oneness of all things."

> "I think differently and view everything with a new perspective. My worldview changed everything, as if a veil

was lifted in understanding the nature of everything as a whole."

"I was able to shed many fears and outdated beliefs as I began to emerge from my experiences."

"My entire frame of mind has changed ever since this contact happened. I see things more clearly as far as philosophically and religiously. I am more aware of a greater power."

"These experiences have helped me to expand my consciousness, to think more clearly about the world and about humans, and to wake up to the different realities and dimensions."

"I no longer fear death as I know now that is just a continuation from this reality... This life is basically just a play on the stage."

"I now understand myself as a part of universal consciousness that is linked not only to every being in the universe but also to the entire universe itself."

"I can feel people's energy, I can see peoples' lessons in life, their directions, and each day this awesome understanding grows and grows. Life comes and it goes – everything is always moving."

One NDEr stated that, "It is outside my domain to discuss something that can only be proven by death. For me, however, the experience was decisive in convincing me that consciousness lives on beyond the grave. Death was not death, but another form of life." This newfound belief can put them at odds with family members who may misinterpret an experiencer's confidence in the afterlife.

Collectively, these experiences reflect emotions of awe, respect for the mystery of nature, and a heightened sense of the sacredness of the natural world. It seems as if their ego melts away and a new way of being emerges. Many feel and sense other people, animals, plants and the earth in a different way and come to the realization that we are all connected, as if consciousness exists everywhere and they are somehow connected to everything. The reality they once accepted without question has been irrevocably changed. Once they have made a decision that this is indeed happening in their lives and they are having these experiences, the world as they knew it ceases to be. But the search for validation and integration of their experience can be a daunting process as depicted below:

> *My relationship with my fiancé of four years became increasingly strained. The more I searched for answers and meaning to help me assimilate my experience, the further apart he and I became. It felt like there was no one I could talk to. No one understood what I'd been through and how terribly homesick I was for Heaven. I longed to go back to the light of God. I tried talking to my doctor and was met with a blank stare and his advice that I just forget about what had happened to me.*

Despite the significant and largely positive transcendent aftereffects facilitated by SMEEs, mainstream science regards them as a symptom of a psychological disorder and are thus harmful or undesirable. This is probably due both to the fact that some mystical experiences are caused by a neurological brain disorder such as temporal lobe epilepsy, and because some persons with schizophrenia have experiences which resemble SMEEs. From a scientific materialist point of view, therefore, SMEEs are a pure brain-based event. There is, therefore, no definitive consensus as to precisely what differentiates SMEEs from pathological states, but there appears to be a definite trend toward regarding them as distinct from pathological states which they resemble.

Discussion

The common reports by those who have a SMEE have motivated researchers to ask how such spiritual insights and experiences relate to the scientific view of phenomena that seem to defy scientific explanation (extrasensory perception, interactions with unidentified aerial phenomena and non-human entities, OBE, NDE, synchronicity, reincarnation, and apparitions, among others). The general scientific community, however, contend that no acceptable theory can explain them since they violate known scientific principles. Consequently, they give it very little, if any, serious consideration. And what is especially troublesome is that those who have a SMEE are often accused of having a psychological disorder. This is generally not the case, however, since those who experience this distinctly different reality are generally transformed in a positive way in terms of their personal and philosophical values and viewpoints. Researching the neurocognitive nature that contributes to such experiences, therefore, may help to build psychological models of how stable embodiment emerges from sensory processing which may allow us to better understand aspects of human consciousness.

The association between delusional beliefs and paranormal and/or religious beliefs raises important questions for those who report to have had a SMEE. That is, do SMEEs fall into the area of psychopathology or into the area of enhanced mental health? This is a valid point, as there are similarities between some psychotic or schizophrenic episodes and some aspects of transcendent experiences. There are, however, significant differences between psychoses and mystical experiences. SMEEs, for instance, are usually associated with feelings of joy, serenity, wholeness and love, while psychotic experiences are usually associated with feelings of confusion, fear and judgment by an angry God which increasingly isolates them from society. Thus, while there can be some similarities between the two experiences, they can generally be distinguished. The majority of those who have a SMEE arise from people who are considered to have no psychological disorder.

Given this foundation, there appear to be two overarching questions pertaining to the SMEE: 1) What causes people to have these experiences, and 2) Are people actually seeing a different world or seeing this world differently? I don't have the answers. The similar anecdotal evidence from individuals who describe their SMEE as an interaction with an invisible reality, however, suggest that this possibility cannot be either irrefutably dismissed or accepted as nothing but a brain-based hallucination or a pathological aberration giving rise to a delusion.

Unfortunately, SMEEs are not amenable to objective scientific analysis since they are spontaneous and cannot, therefore, be elicited for study on demand. The apparent absence of such needed analysis leaves open many questions concerning the nature and associated reason why some people have a SMEE. I can't help but wonder, for instance, if a SMEE actually represents the evolution of our species toward the next stage of higher consciousness by unlocking dormant human potentials. This highly speculative and unanswerable question must be asked since studies are showing that SMEEs transform people from their pre-SMEE personalities into more loving and compassionate individuals – a symptomatic outcome inconsistent with psychotic disorders. And so, are people actually seeing a different world or seeing this world differently?

Bob Davis: Internationally recognized neuroscientist; former professor at State University of New York; author of Life after Death: An Analysis of the Evidence *(from which this article is excerpted) and other works.*

2017

NEAR-DEATH VISIONS OF THE FUTURE
Kenneth Ring, PhD

By now most people have heard of the near-death experience (NDE). These out-of-the-body experiences occur when an individual comes close to death as a result of illness or life-threatening accident. In the course of the NDE he may undergo a "life review" during which he seems to reexperience his entire life in a flash.

I have uncovered evidence that a small number of near-death survivors sometimes also see events that they believe will take place in the future. Because at times these perceptions occur in the course of the life-review phase of the NDE, I have dubbed this phenomenon the "flashforward" experience. These flashforward experiences do not necessarily relate to the future of the individual but can relate to public or global events. These might best be called "world previews" or "prophetic" visions.

I have been conducting a special search for such cases, which are relatively rare, as part of my ongoing research into the NDE. This project has been an outgrowth of my work with the International

Association for Near-Death Studies, headquartered at the University of Connecticut at Storrs, where I serve on the faculty. Many of the cases have come from persons who wrote to the association and with whom I then corresponded and conducted interviews. In most cases, especially those that involved global vision, I traveled to various parts of the United States to tape record their accounts, or I arranged for the individuals to come to Connecticut.

Because the number of these visionary cases is small, it is difficult to draw firm conclusions from them. Nonetheless such reports represent a potentially important dimension of the NDE and make for some fascinating case histories.

Personal flashforwards represent the first type of these previsionary NDEs. As I have already noted, these premonitions usually are received during the NDE itself. Sometimes they come as the sequence of visions in the panoramic life-recall works its way up to the survivor's present life, then goes forward in time to reveal what his future will be or might be like should he return to his body and live. (Sometimes the NDE percipient is given a choice of dying or returning to life.) The second type of visionary experience occurs shortly after the NDE is over or else it "pops" back into memory only when the incident that has been predicted takes place.

A case that illustrates several of these features was described to me by a woman who lives in the Midwest. Her near-death crisis occurred when her cervix was torn as she was giving birth to her youngest child in 1959. During her NDE she left her body and met various beings who conveyed knowledge of the future to her. She was told that it was not yet time for her to die. The beings showed her where she would be living and what she would be doing at a time in the distant future. These revelations surprised her since she was shown a town which was not the one to which she expected to move. Then she saw a scene from her future life.

"I was in a kitchen tossing salad, dressed in a striped seersucker outfit," she said. "My hair had streaks of silver in it; my waist had thickened some, but I was still in good shape for an older woman. There was a strong feeling of peace of mind about my bearing and I was in a joyful mood, laughing with my older daughter as we prepared dinner. The younger daughter (the newborn) had gone somewhere with some other children. This daughter was grown up too but still there were some small children involved who were not in the picture at the moment (i.e., in 1959).

"My husband had just come out of the shower and was walking down a hallway wrapping a robe around him. He had put on more weight than I had and his hair was quite silver. Our son was mowing our lawn but both offspring were only visiting. They didn't live with us."

The woman could see, hear and smell just as if she were physically living the scene. "This picture was only a glimpse," she told me, "but it made one huge impression on me. I must have vowed right then to never forget it because I certainly have not."

The woman added that the vision showed her the way she looks today and she maintains that she correctly saw what her grown children would look like. Her elder daughter eventually divorced, and my informant took over the responsibility of helping raise her two children, therefore fulfilling the prophecy that small children would become involved in her family after her own children were grown. The description of the town in which she would live was also said to be accurate.

A correspondent living in the western part of the United States told me of an incident that he experienced when he was 10 years old and living in his native England. An attack of either appendicitis or peritonitis, for which he was rushed to a hospital, catalyzed the NDE. During his operation he underwent a classic out-of-body experience in which he saw his own body; then he traveled to a place where he met white-robed figures who telepathically communicated concerning his future.

This individual's experience is especially noteworthy because of what happened to him after he revived from his NDE. While convalescing he could remember only that he had been instilled with some strange memories concerning future events. He wasn't aware just how they got there, just that they were there. His NDE occurred in 1941 and although these "memories" were quite clear, he simply didn't know what to make of them until quite recently. He "remembered" that he would be married at the age of 28, that he would have two children and that he would live in a certain house. All of this eventually came to pass.

Cases such as these are certainly provocative, and one can appreciate the striking effect they must have on the individuals who experience them. But how do we know that these accounts are true? It is hard to believe that all the people reporting these visionary experiences are either lying or confabulating. But of course, we are dealing with reports that cannot be easily or objectively corroborated. This is a problem we face with any kind of NDE. In rare instances, however, a near-death survivor's claims can be verified by the external events that fulfilled the prophecy. Recently I came across just such a case.

The subject of this unusual incident is a woman I'll call Belle who has lived her entire life in a small southern city. Now in her 50s, she had an NDE in 1971 following a lung collapse and heart failure during surgery. She underwent a prolonged period of clinical death during which she met "spirit guides" who gave her information about the future.

She was even shown a vision of Raymond Moody who, with the publication of his 1975 book *Life After Life,* would pioneer the scientific study of the NDE. This vision heralded a complex series of coincidences.

Approximately 18 months after Belle's NDE, Moody, who was then beginning his medical studies, moved to the city in which Belle had grown up. He and his wife Louise moved right onto the same street! But since the Moodys lived at the other end of the block, years passed before they knew each other.

On Halloween night 1975 Belle wasn't feeling well, so she asked her husband to take care of the trick-or-treaters. She specifically requested that he not call her to the door no matter how cute a youngster's costume might be. Meanwhile, down the block, Louise Moody was getting ready to take her oldest child Avery out on his Halloween adventure. Although Raymond asked his wife not to take Avery to any strange houses, the two Halloweeners ended up at Belle's place.

And when the Moodys arrived on Belle's doorstep, her husband ignored his wife's request.

"Belle," he called out, "you told me not to call you, but you've got to see this one."

Reluctantly responding, Belle came to the door. Normally she wouldn't have asked a child where he or she came from – she knew most of the neighborhood children anyway – but the Moody youngster caught her interest.

"What's your name?" she asked.

"I'm Raymond Avery Moody, the third," he said.

At that moment the memory of her NDE vision came to mind. "I need to talk with your husband!" she blurted out to Mrs. Moody.

Louise, somewhat taken aback, said, "Oh, did you have one of those experiences Raymond is writing about?"

Belle, who had no idea who Raymond Moody was or what "those experiences" were, couldn't answer this question. She knew only that she had to talk with him. It all became clear only after Louise explained her husband's interest in near-death experiences.

Dr. Moody and Belle met soon afterward and an account of Belle's experience appears in Moody's *Reflections on Life After Life* (1977). Significantly, *Life After Life* had not yet been published when they met in 1975. It was still at the printers and Belle herself had no idea that she had just met the man whose name was destined to become synonymous with the study of NDEs.

The next category of NDE future visions consists of prophetic previews of world events. The remarkable thing about these visions is that they are highly consistent between subjects.

Most NDE percipients who report prophetic visions claim that they received the information about the future during an encounter with guides or a "being of light." In a few instances, however, the visions seem to unfold after the actual NDE. In these cases, it isn't clear whether or not the information was encoded during the NDE. In any event, most of those NDE survivors who have described such prophetic visions have said or implied that they were given far more information than they can recall. Several maintain they were told that they would be given access to some of this hidden information only when and if it was needed.

The content of these visions varies from person to person. A number of these persons have said that the knowledge of a specific event resurfaced one or two days before the prophesied incident took place. One of my informants "predicted" the Three-Mile Island disaster in just this manner. The subject suddenly became aware that a problem would arise at the plant and told at least one other person about the prediction. Other individuals have experienced a sudden recall when the precognized event took place and they remembered that the information had been given to them during their NDE. A visit to a geographical location where a future event was to take place has also triggered the NDE recall. Perhaps most interesting of all are the stories told by persons who have seen visions of the world's future.

I have already mentioned that these broad outlines of our world's future are much the same among the various NDE accounts I have collected. They reveal a consistent pattern. But I must emphasize again that the number of prophetic vision cases in my collection is very small; therefore, any conclusions to be drawn from them must remain provisional.

The following summary, given to me by a man whose vision was part of an NDE in 1943, is typical of this type of global prophecy:

> *Our period of trouble has begun, it seems, certainly as far as the elements are concerned. I think you can expect to see some of the most disastrous upheavals between now and 1988 that we have had in recorded history. The eruption of [Mount] St. Helens is an example. This will not only be in the elements but in the breakdown of interpersonal relationships, between man and man, man and family and nation and nation... My own impression is that we are not facing the end of the world but that we are facing a great deal of upheaval until we have learned to stop being so materialistic and turn to the job He gave us of truly learning to love ourselves and one another.*

Compare this to the account of a woman who had her NDE in 1967 when she was only 16 years old:

> *The vision of the future I received during my near-death experience was one of tremendous upheaval in the world as a result of our general ignorance of the 'true' reality. I was informed that mankind was breaking the laws of the universe and as a result of this would suffer. This suffering was not due to the vengeance of an indignant God but rather like the pain one might suffer as a result of arrogantly defying the law of gravity. It was to be an inevitable educational cleansing of the earth that would creep up upon its inhabitants who would try to hide blindly in the institutions of law, science and religion. Mankind, I was told, was being consumed by the cancers of arrogance, materialism, racism, chauvinism and*

> *separatist thinking. I saw sense turning to nonsense and calamity, in the end, turning to providence.*
>
> *At the end of this general period of transition, mankind was to be 'born anew,' with a new sense of his place in the universe. The birth process, however, as in all the kingdoms, was exquisitely painful. Mankind would emerge humbled yet educated, peaceful and, at last, unified.*

The above two examples are only summaries of typical prophetic vision cases. By examining them more closely, however, we can see certain specific patterns emerge. Most of my informants believe that they have been imbued with total knowledge of the future, even if they cannot easily recall what they were told. Specific themes crop up time and again. One emphasis is on geological upheavals, with special focus on future cataclysmic earthquakes, volcanic activity and landmass changes. Other near-death survivors have spoken about major meteorological changes which will play havoc with our weather. They also speak of a breakdown of the world's economic system.

What about the possibility of a nuclear war? The accounts indicate that the chaos in the world's economic and geophysical conditions will bring us to the brink of war. But the NDE survivors with whom I have spoken do not seem to agree as to whether there actually will be a war, only that the prospect of one (or of a major nuclear accident) will be enormously heightened during the latter part of the 1980s. Two of my informants did indeed believe a war would occur. One said it would start in the Middle East and another reported it would occur in April 1988. Other near-death survivors tell a story in which nuclear energy will be misused and illegal underground testing will occur; but they claim this will not necessarily end in war. Widespread devastation will result from this folly nonetheless.

But there is a happy ending to all this talk of cataclysms, chaos and war. Many near-death visionaries talk of a new era of peace and brotherhood which will emerge from these disasters. In fact, my correspondents usually interpret these disasters as a purging process which will prepare humanity for this new age. Just as the individual who has an NDE may have experienced pain and suffering before personal transformation.

What can we conclude about such experiences? Is mankind really being given previews of world and/or personal events?

Because of the abundant evidence attesting to the reality of precognition, it is conceivable to me that the kinds of phenomena my informants report, including visions of their own futures and the future of the world, offer potentially important information. This seems fairly simple when we analyze flashforward experiences; either the predicted events occurred, or they did not. Belle's vision of Dr. Moody certainly affirms the validity of Belle's experience. The issue is more complex when we turn our attention to prophetic vision cases which are more nebulous and therefore less clearly defined. Either these experiences are showing us our future, or we must find another explanation for them.

One alternative theory is that these prophetic visions may be of psychodynamic origin. In other words, some near-death survivors are simply projecting their own fears about the future (or their unconscious conflicts) onto the world scene. A variant of this theory proposes that an individual may use his personal close call with death as a basis for projecting and experiencing a vision of the "death of the world." In other words, since he as an individual is dying, he somehow transforms this fact into the notion that "the world is dying."

Although superficially plausible, this theory has flaws. The fact that all the prophetic visions I have collected seem to follow certain patterns makes a simple psychodynamic interpretation an unlikely answer. One might expect to encounter a greater variety of projected global futures; yet only one general picture seems to surface. The psychodynamic theory is suspect also because it cannot explain the ultimate vision of peace and beauty that people in the throes of their close calls with death so often report.

A second explanation might be that this picture is being drawn from the current cultural zeitgeist. As we approach the end of the current millennium, more and more attention is being paid to the idea of eventual worldwide destruction and devastation. Never before have the people of the world shown so much concern over the possibility of nuclear war and other world cataclysms. Is it not possible then that some near-death survivors are simply incorporating into their experience what so many others are thinking and feeling? This seems a more likely interpretation of prophetic vision NDEs, although the idea that these people really have seen the future of the world cannot be ruled out.

At this point it is impossible to determine just what lies at the root of these visions. Prophecy? Projected fear? Zeitgeist? Archetypal imagery? Take your pick.

But before we can answer these questions with any certainty, we must find more NDE cases in which prophetic visions and precognitive experiences have played a role. Then we will be in a position to document the existence of such predictions in advance – before the allegedly predicted event takes place. This of course would solve the problem of the unsupported retrospective claim in which the individual asserts he foresaw an occurrence but announces the prediction only after its "fulfillment."

This article is based on a paper, "Precognitive and Prophetic Visions in Near-Death Experiences," from the June 1982 issue of Anabiosis, *the journal of IANDS. It has been adapted by the editors of* FATE *with the help of Dr. Ring.*

Dr. Kenneth Ring: Professor of psychology at the University of Connecticut; a cofounder of the International Association for Near-Death Studies and editor of the association's journal, Anabiosis; *served on the executive board of the Association for Transpersonal Psychology; author of numerous articles, papers and books about NDEs.*

[Editor's note: IANDS is now based in Durham, North Carolina.]

FATE December 1982

IN THE SHADOW OF DEATH
PMH Atwater

I was raised in a police station. That's because my father was a police officer and since we lived outside town on an acreage, Dad would often ferry me back and forth during coffee breaks or whenever he could sign off. I frequently waited around in the station house when he was too busy for chauffeuring, which afforded my insatiable curiosity an "open door" to the bizarre and the ridiculous.

If I happened to be in his patrol car when an emergency arose, I would be whisked along to the scene with strict instructions for my behavior and the need for secrecy. This allowed me to witness the extremes of life at an early age. During this time, my father took it upon himself to train me in the art of observation, drilling me on being alert for minute details and nonverbal cues.

What I didn't observe personally, I read about by scanning daily logs, arrest reports and police files. Later it was deemed illegal in Twin Falls, Idaho for passengers such as me to accompany on-duty police officers or to have free access to police information, but during my youth no such ordinance existed.

Among what caught my attention then was the frequency of cases involving "pre-knowledge," by which I mean incidents where victims claimed to somehow know or sense in advance what was about to happen before it did. This kind of response was especially common with assaults, rapes and muggings. When questioned afterwards, these people would say things like, "I had a feeling not to walk up those stairs alone but there seemed no reason not to so I did," or "I knew if I opened that door something bad would happen but I told myself it was just my imagination," or "I felt creepy all over and real scared because I knew good and well what was going to happen next."

Comments like these puzzled me as a youngster, for I couldn't understand why people who knew about danger in advance would disregard that knowledge and allow themselves to be hurt. It seemed idiotic to me that people who knew better pretended that they didn't. These "victims" usually groaned a lot afterwards, rambling on about how they should have listened to that inner voice or paid attention to that dream or hunch. Then they would pull an about-face and promptly conclude that to acknowledge any such "mental imaginings" was beneath the maturity of a grown adult, that no one in his right mind pays attention to premonitions, anyway. And so the dialogue between police officer and victim would continue, with me shaking my head in disbelief wondering if there was some way I could avoid adulthood when I grew up.

Strange as it may seem, this preknowledge or advance sensing was also true for those who lost their lives, either by accident or by violent assault. Conversations with survivors and next of kin would reveal intriguing stories about how the deceased must have known what was coming because of the way he behaved before the tragedy occurred. It seems that those who died unexpectedly, regardless of how, changed behavior which was normal for them about three to six months before their deaths.

This change would center on a need to wrap up business and personal affairs, seriously and deliberately, as if there existed some unspoken reason for expediency. Insurance policies took on importance, as did the need to visit loved ones and to be more intimate or philosophical than usual. One last "fling" was often enjoyed before the individual would relax and be at peace. Just before the death event, the victim would seem to "glow" as if something important were about to happen, something the individual had prepared for.

Sometimes this pre-knowledge would be more than a series of behavior changes, but also verbal and upfront. One such example which I researched is the case of a woman in her late 20s who was killed in an early-morning automobile pileup on the highway outside Jackpot, Nevada. During the investigation that followed, relatives all told the same story – that the woman knew she was going to die, even how and when. Starting six months before, she had a recurring dream which accurately depicted her later demise. Because of the dream, she had been getting her life in order and telling others what would happen. No one believed her. After the accident, her loved ones and friends were grief-stricken all the more by their refusal to give the woman the benefit of doubt while she was yet alive.

Another incident involved a high school senior who calmly told her parents she would die in a violent accident the day before graduation. This news was nearly a year in advance and the announcement sent her parents into a near-frenzy of worry until they convinced themselves their daughter must be mentally unbalanced. She was sent to several psychologists for evaluation, but each time released with the admonition, "Make certain she takes this drug as it will relax her." There was no dream, no reason for the daughter to make such a statement. "I just know," she'd say, as she readied herself to die.

True enough the day before graduation, she and a girl friend were sitting in a car waiting at an intersection for the light to change when another car suddenly careened out of control and slammed headlong into theirs, killing both girls instantly, yet injuring no one else. Investigators discovered a note written by the daughter revealing that she knew her best friend would be killed at the same time in the same accident as she would. They also discovered that the other girl had displayed the kind of behavior changes which were indicative of someone who knew death was coming even though she had said nothing to anyone about any such awareness.

A year later both mothers each had a dream in which their deceased daughters returned for a visit to explain the why of what had happened. This visitation was so vivid neither mother could keep it to herself. One of them confided in a local astrologer. Ironically the other mother had shared her story with the same astrologer. Becoming excited about the two dreams, the astrologer contacted the psychologist of the first mother, the one most burdened with grief, for advice on how to handle the situation.

Suffice it to say the psychologist then arranged a meeting where all four parents and he could hear each mother describe her dream. Because of this gathering, an incredible healing occurred, and much guilt and grief were released. Neither set of parents knew each other before the meeting; yet each mother experienced her daughter's visitation on the same night at about the same time with the same explanation from the daughters – both girls had agreed before birth to participate in the violent death event for the purpose of one's helping the other work through a lingering fear of dying in that manner. This death scenario was the only reason each girl gave for having incarnated when she did.

Throughout the 20 years that I was married to a farmer, who became an aerial crop duster, there were many occasions when we found ourselves privy to or involved in accidents and death events.

A neighbor who lived just up the road from where we farmed suffocated when a stack of chopped hay fell on him, while another met his death beneath an overturned tractor. Both widows related similar stories about how different their husbands had been acting for several months prior to dying. Each man had quite suddenly become unusually serious and determined to finish everything possible, from paying off debts and securing finances to frequently double-checking with his wife making certain she understood what to do should he not be present. It was spooky, each wife remarked, even eerie. Although neither man had ever discussed the prospect of death, both had displayed the behavior of a person who must have sensed or known what was coming. In each case this behavior change was evident four months in advance.

Both of these men died within a short time of each other, their deaths deeply affecting my husband and me. Even though each incident was different, to us it was as if we were held witness to the same story told in the same manner by the same people. Repetitive similarities were that striking.

This inspired us to begin a research project whereby we would seek out the bereaved of accident victims to determine just how common this advanced "knowing" was. No matter how blank our expressions or how open our questions were, we encountered the same basic pattern. Even children, from the age of four on, exhibited the same or similar cues as adults.

One such case involved a 10-year-old boy who was struck dead by a freakish bolt of lightning while he was playing on a street in the town of Filer with friends. No one else was hurt. There was no storm present.

I knew the boy's mother and we spoke at length about her son's death. She was oddly prepared for the tragedy. Although her son, the oldest of three children, had always been mature for his age, two months before the accident he became strangely deliberate and insistent in his mannerisms, wanting to protect his parents and siblings, being unusually affectionate, understanding and helpful. He seemed obsessed with finishing off jobs yet undone and held in-depth conversations about the meaning of life. Just before he was killed, his behavior reversed to a more relaxed yet expectant mood, as if he were waiting for something important to happen. Classmates noticed the same changes, as did the boy's teacher and grandparents.

Since my husband was an ag pilot, many of our friends were pilots and shared the same dangers of flying. In Idaho, because bees are protected by law, pilots spraying potent chemicals cannot take off until after bees retire for the night and must finish with their work before bees are active again in the morning. Most crop work, then, is done between the hours of 6 PM and 6 AM. Planes are equipped with powerful lights for illuminating broad expanses, and ground crews use bright flashlights to signal pilots as they step off each field row about to be sprayed.

But night flying is made truly complicated by the fact that throughout southern Idaho and eastern Oregon most farm fields are bordered by rural utility lines plus single rows of trees, usually tall poplars which comprise windbreaks. Silos and farm buildings also represent obstacles, making even daylight flying a hazard. A skilled pilot will fly several feet off the ground for the field's length, then lift the plane's nose in time to avoid collision with whatever objects or lines might border the field, circle around and descend sharply for another run. Large fields are navigable but smaller ones, especially if lined on all four sides, are virtually impossible to fly. My husband was one of the few ag pilots who specialized in flying fields other pilots would avoid.

Many of our friends were not only agricultural pilots but also corporate, highway construction and flight instructors, and a number of them died in fiery crashes. One such crash took the lives of three of our friends when the Lear jet they were flying nose-dived into the mesa outside Boise. No one could figure out how the crash occurred since the air was calm and vision unrestricted, so it was later chalked up to "pilot error."

Another crash involved a mid-air collision at midnight over a farmhouse near Adrian, Oregon. Both pilots plus the farmer's wife in the house below were killed. The woman was trapped inside when burning wreckage fell from the planes and set the house ablaze. According to surviving kin, each one of these six people displayed pre-knowledge or the advance behavior changes already noted, although nothing verbal was ever said.

After a decade of nosing around, we finally concluded our investigative quest, having satisfied ourselves that death is no accident no matter how it comes, when it occurs or to whom. We were unable, however, to isolate any recognizable pattern for the inner workings of nonfatal accidents and what constitutes free will versus fate.

Years later I researched reincarnation, metaphysics, mysticism, altered states of consciousness and the so-called paranormal, becoming in the process a professional hypnotist specializing in past-life regressions. While engaged in private practice for six years, I was able to explore all manner of alternate realities, thought forms, fantasy, psychological dramas and what appeared to be actual lives lived before birth in the present one. Each regression was detailed, precise and meaningful to the experiencer, even though I questioned the validity of many of them.

Eventually these sessions became so dynamic and challenging that I discarded convention in favor of the unexpected. This taught me never to assume or deny anything and to remain open and receptive at all times. Skepticism is healthy but in excess can block discovery.

It was during this phase of my work that I surprisingly encountered what I came to call the human soul. My client would be "under" when suddenly a force would take over. There was no mistaking it with any purported past life, present life or aspect of the client's personality. There would be a certain voice change (always the same with each client) and the room temperature would rise when it emerged.

Others present would note a special aura or glow radiating from the client as the voice spoke.

The soul that came forth, no matter from whom, would be detached, loving, objectively knowledgeable – a limitless and timeless source of information. It would speak calmly, confidently and gently. Advice and comments would be offered, for either the prostrate client, me or anyone else who might be in need. Sometimes discourses would ensue on life and its meaning, effective discourses which seemed awesome and sacred. This force, always dependable and unassuming, was nameless, regardless of client, and had no identity of its own. It was never born and did not die. Human deaths, it would say, are planned before birth, and nothing is accidental. Free will is defined as our ability to manipulate the consequence of movements in the earth plane and responses to that activity. Not every session produced such an emergence but those that did were special to say the least.

The day came, however, when I closed my practice. Prospective clients seemed more interested in finding something to blame their troubles on than in truly searching for deeper meaning in their lives. The possibility of contacting their own souls did not interest them. I respectfully referred them to other hypnotists and shut my door to the experience.

For me it was time to pursue other avenues of thought and begin my own spiritual quest. That was 1975. Two years later I physically died, not once but three times, and experienced a different near-death episode with each event.

The first death occurred January 2, 1977 and was caused by a miscarriage followed by severe hemorrhaging. The second, two days later, was from a major thrombosis in the right thigh vein which dislodged, followed by extreme phlebitis. Then, on March 29, I committed emotional suicide; I willed my body dead and it was too exhausted to argue. My home at that time was in Boise. Physicians were not contacted until after the fact, so there is no proof I ever died. The physical condition of my body after each event suggests I must have died and a medical doctor confirmed that suspicion.

The term "near-death experience" was unknown to me when all this happened, nor had I heard of Elisabeth Kübler-Ross, Raymond Moody or Kenneth Ring, the three pioneers who opened up and established the near-death phenomenon as a real incident which deserved professional attention and serious research. Then, I only knew something unusual had happened, something I was not prepared for, and there were aftereffects. Life suddenly became curiously strange, and me with it. This was both a nightmare and a blessing, for coming back to life meant tackling the depths of fear and the heights of love simultaneously.

My case is unique not only because of what happened to me but because of what I did about it. After moving to Washington, DC, I set about on my own quest to seek others as myself, for I had a lot of questions to ask. I wanted to know what others went through and were still facing and how they managed to cope.

This quest took me through 10 states where I spoke with several thousand people and contacted in the process over 200 other near-death survivors. Sometimes I shared my own story to find them; sometimes I gave classes and workshops about what death had taught me; sometimes I simply "bumped" into them as part of the daily routine. After another move and a job change, my employment shifted to one of constant travel where I met still more near-death survivors.

I learned a lot in doing this. Mostly I learned how normal I was for what I had been through.

Nothing more would have ever come from this quest had it not been for Kenneth Ring who, after tracing me through a small publication I had written, asked that I write an ongoing series of articles focusing on the survivor's viewpoint for *Vital Signs* magazine, then published by the International Association for Near-Death Studies in Storrs, Connecticut. After I went on to publicly disclose a brief rendition of what I believed were the patterns of aftereffects, he encouraged me to write a book. This venture would require much research, but the idea that others might benefit from what had helped me spurred me on. *Coming Back to Life* was published five years later in April 1988.

Although the book tackles a broad gamut of subjects, it also devotes a section to the coming of full death where I put together a lifetime of observations to produce what I feel is the pattern of advance behavior cues, usually nonverbal and subconscious, that the one about to die "knows" what will soon happen.

The advance behavior pattern I have observed in most people who die unexpectedly is:

- About three months to three weeks in advance of the death event, the individual involved begins to change his normal behavior in such a manner as to become more serious, determined and oftentimes deliberate in a need to complete unfinished projects or concerns.
- Subtle at first, these behavior changes also center on reassessing affairs and life goals, wrapping things up and putting business in order.
- Simultaneously there can be a desire for deeper, more philosophical discussions. Religion and/or spirituality can become more important, as well as the desire to forgive and forget.
- This is usually followed by a need to see everyone who means anything special. If visits are not possible, the individual will often write lengthy letters or call on the phone.
- As time draws near, individuals usually become quite precise about straightening out affairs and/or training or instructing a friend or relative to take over should anything happen. This instruction can involve details such as finances, insurance policies, inheritance and the completion of goals or projects. Financial matters and the management of personal and private affairs become quite important.
- There is a need, almost a compulsion, to reveal secret feelings and deeper thoughts, to say what has not been said, especially to loved ones. There is also a desire for one last fling or a visit to special places to do what is most enjoyed.
- The drive to settle affairs and wind up life's details can become so obsessive as to appear strange or weird to others. Many times, individuals want to talk over the possibility of "What if I die?" as if they had a dream or premonition. On occasion, such people may appear morbid or unusually serious.

- About 24 to 36 hours before the death event, the individual involved relaxes and is at peace. Because of unusual alertness, confidence and even a sense of joy, he may appear euphoric and exude a peculiar strength and positive demeanor, as if something important was about to happen and all prior preparations were finished.

Some near-death survivors have an inkling that something is about to happen but, for most, there is no hint at all. Even for those who did sense something, the near-death experience still comes as an unexpected surprise.

A typical example is George A.R., a near-death survivor from Hamilton Square, New Jersey, who detailed his experience to show how he came to believe that he could not possibly have died because of the strange way events arranged themselves before his near-death episode happened.

The day before George had an opportunity to buy a burial plot but refused. Because of unexpected car trouble, his wife made a quick trip home and found George perplexed by a seemingly simple pain. The pain was not unusual, but for some reason which George couldn't explain, he insisted upon being taken straight to the hospital, a reaction quite out of character for him. He had his heart attack in the Cardiac Care Unit with a doctor at his side, and while he was out, he heard his wife telepathically calling him through the voice of another and he followed her voice back. Afterwards he clearly saw his brother physically standing at the foot of his bed, when his brother was not in the room at all, verifying for George the reality and importance of the whole episode.

Because near death is a surprise and full death is usually either expected, sensed or somehow known, I have come to realize that the phenomenon of near death is not quite as advertised. Rather it has all the trappings of something else – an experience parallel to death but separate from it, an experience which affords the individual involved a chance to "begin again."

Near death is not full death. I have found the two related but not the same.

It wasn't until I wrote *Coming Back to Life* that I came to realize how much my life has evolved around the death experience. I have been able to view this subject from differing angles, enabling me to regard birth as a time of entry and death as a time of exiting whatever dimension we happen to be inhabiting at any given time. I have also come to realize there are more dimensions and aspects to what is termed "reality" than any person, book, philosophy or religion can define.

PMH Atwater: Writer, author and internationally recognized expert on near-death experiences.

FATE September 1988

FLIGHT TO THE AFTERLIFE
Freda Quenneville

My mother, Judy Herbert [a pseudonym], was a wonderful woman but because she had been plagued with ill health, alcohol problems and suicidal tendencies, there remained much unresolved anguish in my heart about our relationship. Her death occurred in Macon, Georgia on June 12, 1951, when I was 14. Three years later I left the South to live in the Northwest.

In the early afternoon of October 3, 1971, as I lay on my bed resting, the ceiling of the bedroom dissolved, revealing the sky beyond. As the scene shifted I saw an airport landing strip where a ramp was being rolled up to a plane. A young man in flashy white clothes stepped down the ramp. He was blond and striking, with an air of energy and professionalism akin to that associated with an entertainer or stage personality.

Smiling broadly, he greeted and escorted a middle-aged but youthful-looking man up the loading ramp. When I focused my attention on the older man, I was startled to see that he looked like my brother Charles.

When they were seated in the airplane (which was small and round – the kind you see in old cartoons), they flew over the opening in my bedroom ceiling. As the plane circled overhead, the two men waved and smiled, motioning me to join them. No sooner had I agreed to go with them than I found myself inside the airplane.

Although I wondered who this flashy-looking man in white was and why my brother was with him, we did not speak. The man who appeared to be my brother kept looking at me, grinning playfully. Everything felt warm and friendly and a kind of electrical energy emanated from the man in the white clothes.

Quickly the plane reached its destination and as the three of us stood on a flat, desolate plain stretching as far as the eye could see, I became aware of the figure of a woman approaching slowly from the distance. Walking with labored steps, head down, shoulders sagging, this figure was a vivid representation of isolation, despair, hopelessness. My heart felt heavy with her grief. But as she drew nearer, I recognized her as my mother, wearing a navy-blue dress I remembered well and looking some 12 years younger than her age at the time of her death.

The man who looked like my brother broke from us and ran toward her. When she looked up and recognized him, she said with surprise and relief, "I'm glad to see you. I've been so lonely here."

My sad feelings turned to joy at seeing my mother after so many years. I was jumping with excitement, trying to communicate with her, but she gave no indication that she was aware of my presence. My mother and brother, arm in arm, faded into the horizon. The young man in white remained beside me, smiling.

Suddenly I was back in my bedroom, starting to realize that the flashy-looking man had been someone who conducts people over to the "other side." If what I had experienced was real, my brother had died and gone to join our mother. Since all my relatives were in the South and our contacts were infrequent, I had had no recent news warning me of any illnesses or problems.

When I related this experience to my husband, Paul, I struggled to explain the fact that, although the person who had died certainly looked like my brother, he had been different in ways I couldn't pinpoint. Besides, Charles was just 42 and, I thought, in good health.

But I couldn't shake the feeling that my vision had been a glimpse of the afterlife. As the day went on, I grew increasingly concerned about my brother. Around seven o'clock that evening the phone rang. I could tell it was long distance and my body steeled itself for the news. It was my brother's wife.

"This is Mary," she said. "Now I know we don't call often and you'll be worried about Charles, but it's your Uncle Henry. He passed on earlier today. We just got the call from Florida."

This solved the problem in identification – it had not been my brother but my mother's brother. The two men looked very much alike.

This experience left me with some interesting questions to ponder. Had the elaborate symbolism of the airplane been somehow necessary to bridge the "distance" between Florida and the Northwest? Did I need to see events unrolling like a movie so that I could accept them and participate? And had my mother, because of her state of consciousness (she died in a coma), been trapped for the past 20 years in that solitary void? Was that her purgatory, her self-created illusion of suffering brought forward from her days on earth? Was she released only when joined by her brother to whom she had been close?

Two years later my mother appeared to me in a dream. I could hear her beg forgiveness for the wrongs she had caused in my life and ask God to "send blessings to that poor baby." That dream, filled with the love I had yearned for from my mother, was apparently a final parting as she was taking leave of earthbound consciousness. I have had no further awareness of her in the years since then.

Three and a half years after the airplane vision, while I was involved with a theosophical group in Seattle, I became acquainted with a person whom I knew only as Moss. He resembled the flashy-looking man who had orchestrated my uncle's journey after death. In casual conversation he claimed that he sometimes worked as an invisible helper. I related how, with the aid of a helper, I had visited my mother. I told him he reminded me of that person, only he was not so flashy a dresser or as much a showman.

He replied that when out of the body he had a more dazzling appearance from the energy he put into the work.

I was never entirely convinced that he was the man in white on the plane ride. There was, after all, no way to verify such a fantastic possibility. When I asked him if he was indeed the man I saw, he only smiled.

FATE February 1986

THE PORTAL AT GROUND ZERO
Joyce Keller

Sometime during the period that the World Trade Center was under construction, I had a conversation with a psychic who was familiar with the construction site. He looked me straight in the eye and said, "I know that you are occasionally in the area where the World Trade Center is being built. I strongly suggest that you do not ever go into those buildings."

When I asked him why, he said, "Those buildings are cursed from great human suffering. They will definitely come down in our lifetime. Stay away from the area."

His message felt accurate, but of course, my prayer was that it would not be true. My husband, Jack, and I went into the World Trade Center on many occasions. I had mixed feelings about the buildings. I was overwhelmed with the beauty of the towers, and the fact that going to the top was like flying. You could see in all directions, and it was beyond magnificent being up in the clouds.

However, when I walked down hallways, or went into elevators, I became very upset and felt like crying. In spite of the questionable energy, I loved the buildings. I'd always prayed for the protection of the World Trade Center and its inhabitants. I prayed that if the destruction of the buildings had to occur it would be minimal, with no loss of human life.

Prior to and during the excavation for the World Trade Center and for other construction in the area, the remains of at least 19 Colonial-era African American slaves' bones had been unearthed. In October 2003, they were respectfully re-interred a short distance away. Included in this burial were the remains of other black slaves who had also been discovered near the site in 1991.

Historians report that the African American slaves were brought to lower New York during Colonial days, and horribly mistreated. Young children, teens and adults had been brought here from Africa, forced into heavy labor, tortured and killed. The killings were often done by hanging, mostly in the area now known as the New York Financial Center. They were buried in and around the area of the World Trade Center.

The starvation and mistreatment of the slaves went on for many generations. The area around what we now know as "Ground Zero" festered for centuries with the energy of human beings who were horribly mistreated, tortured, and killed. The energy had never been released, and it became more negative after the Financial Center began to grow and prosper and people lost or gained money. As financial dealings were consummated (some fair, some unfair), the negative energy grew in the area. The area surrounding the World Trade Center became an overwhelming magnet of darkness. The hatred, misery, despair and human suffering had been building up for centuries. It had never been cleansed or released.

Two months before 9/11, Jack and I bought a lovely little apartment in the shadow of the World Trade Center, only 1,000 feet away. The apartment was spectacular, with sweeping views of the New York harbor, the bridges and the Statue of Liberty. On the day that we moved in, Jack and I went to the roof of our building. Jack looked straight up at the World Trade Center as it towered over our building of 40 floors. Looking up at the magnificent edifice, he said, "If, God forbid, those buildings come down, my prayer is that they go straight down, and not over here!" We both laughed weakly, knowing that it was not something we should laugh about.

September 11, 2001 was a clear, unbelievably beautiful day in New York. We had gone back to our house on Long Island, so we were not in Manhattan when the attack occurred. Jack and I stood transfixed and horrified as we watched the morning news and saw the towers as they burned and then collapsed. We watched our little building in Battery Park City become obliterated and completely covered with black smoke.

When the power in our building was turned back on a few weeks later, we returned to our apartment. The air in the city was almost beyond description. There was not only an overwhelming smell of death, but also smoke, plastic desks, paper and God knows what else. People walked with their heads down, most everyone either wearing a mask or covering their mouths and noses with a hanky. People were walking and crying. Since traffic was detoured, we had to walk many blocks. Red Cross volunteers from out of town were at many street corners. Emergency workers put food and water into our hands. People walked like zombies, not able to fully comprehend or accept what had happened to our city, Buses did not charge anyone, taking people wherever they had to go. Volunteers came on board, giving out fruit and water. Most people sat in stunned silence, or quietly sobbed.

When we finally got to our apartment building, we walked in and were greeted by the front desk concierge. He was usually formal, but not this time. He grabbed Jack and me and began crying. "My God, I thought you were both dead. Five people who lived here died in the disaster. I'm happy to see you." We all hugged each other.

When we got up to our apartment, we entered with great trepidation. The power had been off for quite a few days, and we had the usual food supply in our refrigerator. We were very fortunate, though, and happy to find that our building workers had cleaned everything out for us.

Jack and I went up to the roof and stood there, overwhelmed with sadness. Our wonderful World Trade Center was gone. In its place was a big, smoking hole filled with tons and tons of debris. Many workers were going full-steam ahead with the cleanup, still optimistic that some survivors might be found. Rescue dogs were brought in, also courageously scouring the steaming debris for survivors. None were found.

That night, we fell asleep in our apartment with great difficulty. I was asleep only for a short time when I was awakened. I was inspired to walk into the living room. More asleep than awake, I realized that the room was filled with smoke, but it wasn't physical. I also realized that the room was filled with spirits ... mostly firefighters!

Do not be afraid

I walked over to the bay window that faces out to the harbor and the Statue of Liberty. I saw a huge, white cloud of light forming over the harbor. I heard a voice say to me, "Joyce, you have to stand by the window, and direct these departed souls out to the light which has formed over the harbor. There are many spirit teachers and angelic forces waiting to take them into the light, and to where they need to go."

By now, Jack had gotten up and joined me at the window. We stood there for hours, until the sun came up. We continuously said to the spirits who were leaving, "Go this way. Look at the light over the harbor. Go ahead. Don't be afraid. Your loved ones are waiting for you. They will assist you right now. Do not be afraid!"

The line of departed entities seemed endless. They kept coming and coming. Many were World Trade Center employees who wanted to go back to their desks or call their families to tell them they were all right. Many did not know they were no longer in their bodies. Some firefighters joked with us. One fireman said, "Look, I can fly! Even with my boots on!"

Finally, as the sun came up over the harbor, we realized that the line of departed souls was coming to an end. We knew that they had all crossed over. I had a feeling of peace sweep over me and realized that Jack and I were completely exhausted. I looked down at the floor and saw that I was standing in a pool of my perspiration.

The next day, I meditated on the experience. I was told that we had been moved to that apartment and that building for definite purpose. The building is exactly between the World Trade Center and the harbor. God had turned our apartment into what is known as "a portal" or opening to higher realms. We were used as "earth helpers" along with cosmic workers to accomplish the job. Many other earth helpers were also enlisted, some in buildings around the area, and some on the street. My guidance also told me that many children in the area could have died, since this is an area that has many children, but not one was lost.

Remains of the World Trade Center Tower 2 after the 9-11 terrorist attacks. Credit: Wikimedia Commons.

I was also told that I would receive proof within 24 hours that this apartment had been turned into a portal. I was curious about that and couldn't wait for it to happen.

The next day when I was walking the streets of New York City, I noticed many vendors selling photographs of the World Trade Center and Battery Park City. A large photo particularly caught my eye. It showed the World Trade Center as it had looked before 9/11. In the center of this photo was one apartment building that was very hard to miss. It was our building. It is easy to spot, since there is a circle on the top, with what looks like a missing clock. Well, of course, we had to buy the photo. It was so attractive, and only $4.00. When we took it home and got ready to hang it on the wall, Jack called me. He said, "Look at this!" On the back of the photograph were the words "The Portal."

Is the area surrounding Ground Zero cleansed of old, dark, evil energy? Is there residual negative energy? Why did almost 3,000 people die? Was this the balancing of their karma? Were they helpless victims? Or was this the acceleration of their karma, so that the slate was wiped clean in one lifetime, rather than many? Are there other areas like this in our country, or in the world? Can we keep events like this from occurring?

After much meditation, my impression is that, as Edgar Cayce said, "There are no accidents. There are no victims." People, at a certain level of consciousness, understand and usually agree to accept whatever comes their way, after their karma is explained to them. The cell phone messages that were heard by friends and relatives on September 11 are, for the most part, incredibly cool and calm. There was an all-pervasive calmness among the victims, as if they knew what was happening, and agreed to it.

There were many reports of people who worked in the World Trade Center and lived through the experience. Many people could not understand or explain how they were sitting at their desk one minute, drinking coffee and then suddenly standing out on the street in front of the World Trade Center, still holding a coffee cup in their hands. Many people had no memory or awareness of exiting the building and safely making their way out to the street.

September 11 was a tragedy beyond description. However, mixed in with that tragedy are so many blessings. For instance, all the children in Battery Park City's nurseries and schools survived, as did many residents and their pets. Also, there were World Trade Center employees who survived, either because they missed their train or overslept that morning.

The 9/11 experience should be a wakeup call for all of us. We need to appreciate the beauty and blessings of our country. We need to strengthen and empower our God-connection. We need to listen intuitively to our own inner and angelic guidance, which is the God within.

Joyce Keller: Internationally known psychic, bestselling author, radio host and media personality.

FATE August 2006

DYING, DEATH AND SURVIVAL

LIFE AFTER DEATH: HISTORICAL AND NEW EVIDENCE
Rodger I. Anderson

Human beings have long believed that a part of themselves is capable of surviving the deaths of their bodies. Despite this almost universal conviction, critical and systematic efforts to discover whether this belief has any foundation in truth are relatively recent. It was not, in fact, until the latter part of the 19th century that serious research on the subject was initiated with the formation of the Society for Psychical Research in England. Since then the evidence has grown to the extent that even the skeptic can no longer reasonably maintain that there is no case for survival. There is a case, a rather impressive one, that such psychic occurrences as apparitions, deathbed visions and communications received through trance mediums suggest that not all of a person is lost in dying. Whether or not a good case can be made for survival on the basis of such evidence, however, is no longer really the issue in psychical research. The issue is whether the survival theory is the only or best interpretation of these phenomena.

The historical problem

For many years survival researchers have been preoccupied with this problem of alternate interpretations. Take the phenomenon of trance mediumship, for example. Some credible reports show that certain trance sensitives can offer their sitters correct information about a variety of deceased persons. The question, in such situations, is from what source does the medium derive the information. Even after fraud, sensory cues, suggestion and so forth have been ruled out, there is still the possibility that the medium was reading the minds of the sitters. In several instances this is almost surely the correct explanation, such as when the communicator imparts only those items of information known to the sitters, including information that is later found to be erroneous.

But telepathy with the living can by no means adequately explain all cases of alleged spirit return through mediums. For example, in numerous instances the sensitive has volunteered information, wholly unknown to anyone present at the seance, about a deceased person. Sometimes this information has even corrected mistaken impressions held by the sitters about the persons allegedly communicating. Cases also abound in the literature concerning communicators representing persons wholly unknown to anyone present at the time. These entities will sometimes offer a wealth of accurate information that, taken in its entirety, will be beyond the knowledge of any single living person.

Can all these cases be explained as the result of ESP from the sitters or from other living persons to the psychic? Some certainly can, but the third category of cases mentioned above – known as "drop-ins" in the literature – suggest rather forcefully that some persons continue to manifest in characteristic ways after their deaths. Since, however, there are no known limits to what ESP is capable of accomplishing in this world, it remains theoretically possible that the medium came by the information without any aid from purported spirits. The idea that a psychic can use unlimited ESP to gain information to present to her sitters as a message from the dead is called the super-ESP theory, or super-psi.

The history of survival research is the story of the continuing warfare between these two interpretations of the evidence. Although a

Soul leaving the body upon death. Credit: Luigi Schiavonetti, 1808. Wikimedia Commons.

great deal of evidence was accumulated during psychical research's early days – mostly concerning apparitions and contacts with the dead through trance mediums – no evidence that unequivocally proved survival ever emerged. The skeptic could always invoke the telepathic, clairvoyant and even precognitive powers of the medium to explain the evidence.

This idea gained some empirical support when, in 1900, Mrs. Henry Sidgwick reported on a sitting with Leonora Piper, a famous trance medium. In her report Sidgwick described a crucial session in which the sitter conversed with an old acquaintance, one Dr. Wiltse, who stated that he was drowned and his body was in the water. The communicator went on to answer correctly a number of test questions, leaving no doubt that the communicator was speaking as Dr. Wiltse. Later, however, it was learned that Dr. Wiltse was alive and well and undergoing no abnormal experience at the time his "spirit" reported him dead.

Evidence that some communicators, like the reputed "Dr. Wiltse," can volunteer accurate information without being the person they purport to be considerably increases the likelihood that many other communicators are heard because the medium's ESP is directed upon persons or events in this world. For this reason, among others, modern parapsychologists focusing on survival research have concentrated on ways and means of discriminating between the super-psi and survival hypotheses. New cases, new categories of evidence and new ways of conceptualizing the issues involved have arisen within parapsychology since the 1970s. Although still, sadly, the occupation of only a tiny minority of parapsychologists today, their efforts have already resulted in much information that is difficult to reconcile with the view that all evidence for survival is rooted in the paranormal capabilities of still-living persons.

Modern survival research has been proceeding on two broad fronts: research to see if we, the living, are able to survive death and research on direct contact with the deceased. Each of these approaches will be considered in turn.

Survival research with the living

Clearly, unless we have reason for believing that the "self" is not restricted to the body, to talk of someone's "surviving" death makes little sense. If, however, some aspect of the mind can extend beyond the body during life – perhaps by visiting distant scenes where it can be detected by others – then there is much more likelihood that the "self" is not permanently tied to the body and its fate. In other words, such an occurrence would represent an *a priori* case for survival. Researchers at both the American Society for Psychical Research in New York and the Psychical Research Foundation (PRF) in Durham, North Carolina became interested in this question when they received funding for survival research in the 1970s.

Karlis Osis was in charge of research at the ASPR. His approach was to see if there existed some perceptual element within us capable of leaving the body. He recruited Ingo Swann, a well-known New York psychic, for a series of what turned out to be highly successful experiments. Swann would sit in a chair in an ASPR lab room while attached to a polygraph. Hanging from the ceiling was a box-like apparatus in which two target pictures were placed side by side but with a barrier between them. Swann was asked to "leave his body," send his mind to one side of the box, report what he saw, swing around to the other side and describe the second target picture.

Osis thought that ESP – which does not function like normal perception – would be incapable of such finely-tuned distinctions between the two targets. Perfect success, on the other hand, would indicate that some element of Swann's mind was genuinely functioning apart from his physical body.

Swann performed magnificently on these tests, which were carried out repeatedly. Often his descriptions of the two pictures were so exact that it seemed as if he had looked at them through his physical eyes, although the targets were safely out of his visual range. On one occasion he even complained that he could not properly see the pictures because the light bulb illuminating them had gone out. The experimenters had to use a ladder to prove Swann correct!

Research conducted at the Psychical Research Foundation in Durham proceeded in different directions. Robert Morris, who was in charge of research activities there, was more interested in finding some aspect of the "self" that could leave the body and be detected. He carried out several experiments with Keith Harary, then a young Duke University undergraduate. Harary could "leave the body" at will and Dr. Morris conducted several experiments to see if delicate scientific instruments could detect Harary's traveling self.

The results were curious. Sometimes the instruments reacted when Harary contacted them "out-of-body" but there was no consistency. Better results were produced when Morris and Harary turned their attention to the use of animals as detectors.

The most famous and successful series of experiments concerned a little kitten named, appropriately enough, "Spirit." This kitten, which belonged to Harary, was placed in a special container at the PRF, where she was watched by a co-experimenter. His job was to record when the cat was active or inactive in its small environment. Harary was taken to another building or to Duke University Hospital, where he projected to the cat several times during the course of the experiments. The co-experimenter watched the kitten become remarkably quiet every time Harary projected to it. The kitten's sudden changes in behavior were consistent and obvious. Unfortunately, neither Morris nor Harary had the same luck with other species – not even when they used PRF volunteers as detectors.

Both Osis and Morris came to believe that their experiments were consistent with the survival hypothesis but not proof of it. Morris in particular was not able to determine what his experimental results truly implied.

Parapsychologists, however, rightly demand something more than mere evidence of the bare possibility of survival. The evidence, for them, must directly suggest survival by showing the existence of a component of personality that is both detachable from the body and obviously not dependent upon a functioning nervous system.

For a while it seemed that the best approach to this problem would be by way of the out-of-body experience, but this approach has not proven as helpful as was originally hoped. Although much was discovered about the psychological dynamics of the experience, it was also found that the feeling of being out of one's body is only rarely veridical. For example, even with his remarkable talents, Keith Harary was inconsistent when performing target OBE experiments of the sort Dr. Osis had designed for Ingo Swann. Even Osis later acknowledged that he could find only one other subject capable of performing well on his tests. He tested several others who claimed out-of-body talents but they all failed his experiments.

But the relevance of the out-of-body experience to survival research continues to interest some investigators. Some of the evidence collected in the 1970s indicated – in certain areas at least – that something physically detectable might actually be capable of leaving the body. But this conclusion must remain provisional because many other parapsychologists believe that ESP and PK-at-a-distance can explain even Swann's and Harary's laboratory successes.

Research on near-death phenomena

Research on the out-of-body experience brings us to two other areas that have caught the attention of survival researchers: the near-death experience (which often incorporates an OBE) and apparitions of the living – which are sometimes experienced by the agent as an out-of-body excursion. These latter reports are particularly provocative because of their generic similarity to apparitions of the dead. This has led some to conclude that apparitions of the dead may also be vehicles of consciousness, in precisely the same way an out-of-body experience is. But this is purely an inference, for there exist numerous cases of apparitions of the living in which the ostensible agent had no awareness of ever leaving the body!

The relevance of near-death experiences to survival is even more ambiguous.

FATE readers are familiar with this phenomenon, first brought to wide public notice by Raymond Moody in 1975 with the publication of his book *Life After Life*. Dr. Moody chronicled the accounts of many persons who were, for a brief time, clinically "dead" but who survived to tell the tale. Of those he interviewed, many spoke of out-of-body traveling, meeting their deceased relatives and visiting the "spirit world." Research on the NDE was placed on a more secure foundation when Kenneth Ring in Connecticut and Michael Sabom in Georgia, eschewing the anecdotal approach used by Moody, employed proper sampling procedures to poll near-death survivors. They too found that NDEs are reported by many – although certainly not all – who survive clinical death.

Dr. Sabom took his research a step further by investigating several cases in which his informants correctly described the procedures used to resuscitate them. The remarkable medical and technical knowledge displayed in these accounts led Dr. Sabom to conclude that his informants may actually have left their bodies as they claimed.

Nor has Sabom been alone in his findings. One well-documented case, similar in many respects to those Sabom collected, was placed on record by Kimberly Clark of Harborview Medical Center, Seattle. The case came to light when Clark was counseling a woman recovering from a heart attack. The woman was agitated because of an experience she had undergone while seemingly unconscious. She told Clark she had left her body while being resuscitated. She eventually left the room and ended up on the ledge of another story of the hospital, where she spotted a tennis shoe with a worn toe. The woman beseeched Clark to check out the ledge.

Clark went up to the ledge and spotted the tennis shoe. What particularly impressed the researcher was the way the patient had described the shoe. "The only way she would have had such a perspective," she writes, "was if she had been floating right outside and at very close range to the tennis shoe."

The ubiquity of the NDE has been further confirmed by work with other selected populations. Bruce Greyson, originally working at the University of Virginia, collected a number of NDE accounts from suicide survivors. Nancy Bush at the International Association for Near-Death Studies in Connecticut found several cases reported by children who almost died – a remarkable finding since recent research shows that children between the ages of five and 12 rarely experience conventional OBEs.

Certainly, these experiences are consistent with the survival hypothesis. They are the kinds of experiences that might be expected to occur if we really do survive death. But by themselves they offer little direct evidence for supposing that the near-death experience is a literal journey into the beyond. Researchers who promote the NDE as proof of survival still need to address or clarify a number of thorny issues. For example:

> (1) NDE-like experiences are not limited to persons at or near the point of death. They may also occur while some individuals are undergoing classical "mystical" experiences, using a variety of hallucinogenic drugs or experiencing the effects of certain commonly-used anesthetics. The experience, in other words, can occur in situations in which death is not a prospect, which somewhat undermines the connection of such events to the issue of everlasting life.
>
> (2) A second reason for doubting whether the NDE represents a real journey into the hereafter is that a collection of such cases, while broadly similar, will also contain a number of elements that are rather obviously due to cultural traditions. Some older accounts, for example, contain references to angels with wings, choirs of heavenly hosts or other elements derived from the popular orthodoxy of the time. Those occurring in non-Christian cultures may differ even more dramatically from the type of experiences reported today in the West. Take the story of Er as told by Plato in the *Republic*. Er experienced a near-death episode in which he saw

the souls of the dead choosing their reincarnations, a perspective rarely ever mentioned in current NDE accounts.

In summary, the NDE lacks the consistency we would expect if it were a genuine glimpse into an objective beyond.

Proponents of the NDE argue, however, that, while it is true that NDEs contain a number of "culture-specific" elements, they also possess enough universal features to suggest that something about the experience transcends cultural conditioning. In this respect the NDE is similar to a related class of near-death occurrences – so-called deathbed visions, in which the dying see welcoming figures (often deceased relatives) guiding them into death.

Original research on this subject was undertaken by Karlis Osis back in the 1950s and 1960s. He discovered how widespread deathbed visions are when he surveyed hundreds of doctors and nurses and published his celebrated monograph *Deathbed Observations by Physicians and Nurses.* He could find no medically viable explanation for these cases. During the 1970s Osis conducted a similar study in India and found that cases reported from that culture were little different from those collected in the West. (He reported on his research in his book *At the Hour of Death,* co-authored with Erlendur Haraldsson of Iceland.)

These findings are again consistent with the view that such experiences provide a prevision of things to come. But alternate, and just as logically consistent, theories can account for deathbed visions *and* near-death experiences. The most popular of these theories is that experiences of this sort are broadly uniform because we all feel and react pretty much alike when we confront death and dying.

In terms of Jungian psychology experiences such as the NDE and deathbed visions are "archetypes" – i.e., built-in patterns of response to help people cope with significant life situations. The recurrent types of imagery reported – departed loved ones, marvelous landscapes, religious and mythical figures – are universal symbols of the transformation of death. They provide the dying person with a perfect psychological defense against the very situation that threatens to overwhelm him.

This way of looking at the NDE, it should be noted, does not imply that the experience is necessarily a delusion, a vital lie told by the mind to itself in order to escape an otherwise unacceptable situation. But neither does it mean that the experience is a genuine intimation of immortality.

This kind of theorizing can also explain cases such as those collected by Sabom. Like many other altered states of consciousness that seem favorable to the emergence of ESP, the subject undergoing an NDE or deathbed vision may use ESP to bolster the experience or give added credence to its "reality." Such cases would seem analogous to dreams, which on rare occasion will likewise incorporate features based on precognitive information or telepathically-received messages.

The new evidence

It should be clear by now that survival research with the living can carry us only so far in our effort to answer the question of human destiny after death. Certain individuals may be able to leave their bodies at will, apparitions of the living and dying may continue to appear and people on the threshold of death may report similar visions of a world beyond.

But none of these phenomena really tell us what, if anything, happens to us after the biological death of the body. OBEs, NDEs and kindred phenomena are important to survival research in the same way all the phenomena of parapsychology are important. Such events, when veridical, show that there exists a component of mind not currently comprehensible to science in strictly physiological terms. Unfortunately, these phenomena cannot demonstrate that this component can exist apart from a functioning nervous system, for whatever component may be capable of leaving the body during life may die along with the biological demise of the body.

If, by definition, research with the living cannot provide the kind of evidence needed to prove survival, there remain those types of phenomena that directly suggest the activities of the deceased.

The renewed debate about the super-ESP theory

Although often impressive, few of these cases are inexplicable by the old super-ESP theory. Take the case of an apparition of the dead collectively perceived by several witnesses. This may mean that there is something there to be seen but the apparition may also be the product of a sort of "telepathic contagion" between the witnesses. The same ambiguity attaches to research with trance mediums. Just about all mediumistic "communications," even when highly evidential, can be attributed to the medium's super-ESP. For this reason, many researchers, including the late J. B. Rhine, maintained that we should not ask the survival question until we know more about the limits of ESP in this world. Without knowing these limits, argued Rhine, research on survival can only lead back to the living.

Not all modern parapsychologists have been impressed with this argument, however. While admitting the theoretical possibility that the evidence for survival is really due to the agency of still-living minds, they also stress that we have no right to invoke such a theory for the sole purpose of swallowing up the data most evocative of evidence for survival. They point out – rightly so – that ESP as we see it occurring in the laboratory is a comparatively weak effect, one that is usually detectable only by the use of statistics and other fine measurements. This certainly does not look like the kind of near-omnipotent faculty needed to explain these cases, especially reported with trance mediums, that most forcefully suggest spirit return.

Although there is some tentative evidence that something like "super-ESP" can be employed by certain exceptionally gifted psychics, there is no evidence that this faculty can explain the better cases of postmortem return. So far as we know, for example, ESP – whatever its range and capacity – cannot enable a person suddenly to speak a foreign language he never learned. Yet in a number of recent, well-attested cases such a feat was accomplished – and often over long periods of time.

Xenoglossy and the problem of drop-in communicators

The subject of xenoglossy, speaking a language the subject has never learned or heard, is the special interest of Ian Stevenson of the University of Virginia. He has published several papers and two books on the topic.

The first of these books, published in 1974, dealt with a Philadelphia housewife identified only as Mrs. T. E. During hypnotic sessions undertaken by her husband, an entity began to communicate in a strange language later identified as Swedish. The communicator, who called himself "Jensen Jacoby," claimed to have been a peasant who died during a battle. Several Swedish-speaking witnesses interacted with the entity, whose vocabulary seemed mainly restricted to that of the 16th and 17th centuries. "He" was able even to identify correctly old Swedish artifacts borrowed from a local museum. An extensive search undertaken by Dr. Stevenson failed to uncover any evidence that the subject had ever studied – or had even been exposed to – the language.

Stevenson also recruited a specialist on the language to aid him in his investigation. Dr. Nils Sahlin, a Philadelphia resident who teaches Swedish, testified, "Most remarkable to me was the medium's pronunciation of the words she used, whether ours or her own. She did not speak her Scandinavian as an American would. She had absolutely no difficulty with the *umlaut* sounds or other peculiar Scandinavian sounds and accents."

The Rev. Carroll Jay of Greenbush, Ohio, reported a remarkably similar case in his book *Gretchen, I Am*. This book tells how Mrs. Jay, after being hypnotized by her husband in 1970, became a German-speaking personality named "Gretchen." Stevenson was called in to investigate the case. Because he speaks German fluently, the psychiatrist was able to interview the personality directly. Mrs. Jay, as Gretchen, told of her life in 19th-century Germany in some detail, although most of her claims could not be verified. Stevenson nonetheless felt that the entity was capable of making creative use of the German language, even if she often spoke it badly. He also undertook an investigation into Mrs. Jay's background and could find no evidence that she ever studied the language.

Unfortunately, both subjects were at least once detected in circumstances suggesting they were not above using normal means to bolster their psychic abilities. But Stevenson felt that these rudimentary incidents of possible bad faith cannot account for the linguistic complexities of the cases.

In many respects the most impressive of Stevenson's xenoglossy cases comes from India and concerns an educated woman living in Nagpur. While entranced she "becomes" another woman who died over a century ago in another part of the country. The subject of this ongoing investigation is Uttara Huddar, who normally speaks several languages and who works in the field of education. Yet while she is spontaneously entranced, she becomes a girl who calls herself Sharada and who speaks only Bengali – a language distinct from any of those known to Uttara in her waking state. It is also impressive that Sharada has offered many obscure details, which have invariably turned out to be true or at least plausible, concerning her life.

Of course, the critical problem with these and other xenoglossy cases is the issue of exactly what we are dealing with. Are they cases of postmortem return, "possession," reincarnation or some kind of really super-ESP? Except for the last, though, each of these possibilities still points to survival after death.

Cases such as the above are especially provocative because the subjects had *no obvious talent for ESP except when controlled by a specific discarnate agent*. So where did their suddenly-acquired skills come from? Some speculate that "imagined" control by the dead somehow acts to "boost" the subject's innate capacity for displaying psychic abilities. But if this were so, it is worth asking ourselves why most successful sensitives or trance mediums in the Spiritualist tradition cannot do the same? By and large, the most impressive cases of this type seem to occur in reincarnationist settings, where there is more of an apparent "fusing" of personalities than is commonly the case in the kind of trance mediumship practiced in the West. Perhaps – this is only a suggestion – the kind of deep "possession" that may be presumed to occur in cases of the reincarnation type allows for a more complete manifestation of the dead than would otherwise be possible.

Another type of mediumistic phenomenon that is difficult to explain away convincingly with the super-ESP theory is "drop-in" communicators. These entities appear uninvited at seances and represent persons previously unknown to anyone present. Sometimes these communicators seem not at all sure who they are, but a significant number offer impressive evidence of personal identity. In some few instances the information volunteered by these entities has been traced to published reports (usually obituaries) that the medium may well have come across in the normal course of events; other cases in the literature, however, cannot be accounted for in such commonplace terms. For example, in some recorded incidents of this kind the facts given by the drop-ins proved correct but had been inaccurately reported in the only printed source of information potentially available to the psychics.

A series of exceptionally interesting drop-in communicators was examined in 1971 by Alan Gauld, a psychologist at the University of Nottingham. His investigation focused on a Ouija board circle operated by a small group of persons in Cambridge. They had formed the group in 1942 and continued to hold regular meetings for many years thereafter. Messages had been received from over 200 entities, of whom most were deceased friends and relatives of the sitters. A number of the communicators, however, had been of the drop-in kind, although the group had made little effort to verify any of the information volunteered by these personages. It was this collection of cases that Dr. Gauld took up many years later when he examined the group's records.

Between 1950 and 1952 a communicator named Harry Stockbridge (a pseudonym used by Gauld to protect the surviving family's privacy) offered several bits of information about himself. No one in the group knew him but the entity related in halting terms that he had been connected to the Northumberland Fusiliers as a second-lieutenant. He had died on July 14, 1916. He also said he was "Tyneside Scottish," tall, dark and thin; his most distinguishing feature was his large brown eyes. He told the group that he hung out in Leicester and that records about him could be found there. He also added some comments about his likes and dislikes.

The original Cambridge group had done little to investigate the communicator's story when Gauld considered it in 1965, 15 years or so after the reception of the messages. By checking military records, the British psychologist learned that a 2nd-Lt. H. Stockbridge of the Northumberland Fusiliers had in fact existed. He had been killed in action on July 19, 1916. Gauld at first thought the communicator was mistaken about the date of his death, but when Stockbridge's actual death certificate was examined, Gauld discovered that *the communicator had been correct and the official military records wrong*. Stockbridge had, in fact, died on July 14. The death certificate also noted that the officer had been born in Leicester (in 1896).

Further detailed research in unpublished military archives showed that before his death Stockbridge had been transferred to a Tyneside Scottish battalion. Gauld also tracked down some of Stockbridge's surviving relatives who verified the physical description the communicator gave of himself.

The case is complicated even further by the fact that two of the Cambridge group had dreams about a "Powis" street during the time the Stockbridge communications were being received. When asked about the street at a subsequent session, the communicator reported he knew it well. Research undertaken in Leicester established that the fallen officer had been born in a home very close to Powis Street in the city.

Gauld noted in his report on the case that only two members of the Cambridge group were operating the Ouija board when the Stockbridge communications came through. According to Gauld, neither of them "had any contacts in Leicester or had ever visited it, and I could trace no likely line of contact between either of them or any member of the Stockbridge family." Nor could Gauld find any published records that contained all of the information given to the Cambridge group.

Other researchers have also been attracted to the study of drop-in communicators. Stevenson especially studied the talents of the late Hafsteinn Björnsson, an Icelandic trance medium. He too was often bothered by drop-ins at his seances. Two of them offered enough information for their identities to be verified through old records that were probably not available to the psychic. (Stevenson's two reports on Björnsson's drop-ins, which he coauthored with Erlendur Haraldsson, appeared in 1975 in the *Journal of the American Society for Psychical Research*.)

It is up to the skeptic to explain in such cases how super-ESP can lock in on a deceased personality known neither to the psychic nor to the sitters. Some critics of the survival theory point out that, in many drop-in cases, the sensitive inhabits the same geographical location as the purported communicator. They posit that the psychic probably picked up the relevant information by means of "psychometry," possibly from the geographical area itself. But can this theory account for the highly specific nature of the information communicated, or explain how the sensitive managed to select – among the thousands of impressions available – just those of one particular deceased individual?

Without doubt the easiest explanation for most verified cases of this sort is to assume that it was the communicator, not the medium, that was responsible for its own appearance. This is far simpler than the cumbersome super-ESP explanation, which makes the selection of the communicator depend upon the occult operation of wholly unknown factors.

New light on apparitions and hauntings

Some apparitions of the dead are hard to explain as the creations of us, the living. The whole subject of apparitions and hauntings has come in for something of a reevaluation among parapsychologists, thanks in no small part to the efforts of Karlis Osis.

Until his retirement from the ASPR, Dr. Osis was particularly interested in cases of the apparitional type that point directly to survival. One case he investigated concerned a reputed haunting, complete with poltergeist-like effects, that persisted for over 10 years. The haunting outlived three sets of the house's owners. No identifiable living agent seemed linked to the case, although there was a rather plausible dead one. The case ended after a visiting psychic performed an exorcism of sorts.

Osis presented his most intriguing case, however, to a parapsychology conference that convened at Fairleigh University in Rutherford, New Jersey in the summer of 1983. The case concerned a businessman Osis identified only by his first name, Leslie, who had died in a plane crash the preceding year. The man's family worried about the impact the news would have on Leslie's aging mother, who was already in poor health. A friend of the family shared this concern. Knowing that Leslie's mother did not believe in life after death, she prayed to the deceased Leslie to appear to his mother as a sign of his survival. Since the man had previously fathered a son who died as an infant, the friend requested in her prayer that the businessman appear along with the child. The friend told no one except her husband about her petition.

Three hours after the friend had prayed for the third time, Leslie's mother awoke from sleep to see her son with his deceased child.

"I was wide awake then," she told Osis. "They were content. They were happy that they found each other, that they were together now. And they were letting me know that it is so. I got that feeling."

The case, thus far, might be attributed to chance or telepathy but these explanations seem somewhat strained in the light of a curious denouement. When he was killed, Leslie left behind a six-year-old niece who lived about 100 miles from his home. She did not know the family friend who had prayed to Leslie, but she too saw the apparitions. Three hours before Leslie's mother saw the figures, the little girl awoke from sleep to see a cloud in her room. Within it she saw Leslie and his son holding hands.

It is difficult in cases such as these to imagine what was going on if the dead were not somehow involved, or at least some entity capable of acting on its own initiative. Nor is Osis' case unique in the literature of phantasmal appearances. Some of the cases collected by the early SPR workers reported these ephemeral forces appearing to people with whom they had no special connection. No good reason seems viable for these visitations if they were only being generated by the minds of the percipients.

There are also on record a small number of curious incidents wherein the ghost of a long-deceased person appeared to a perfect stranger. In doing so, the ghost disclosed many obscure items of information later found to be correct, and probably known only to the deceased person. Cases of this sort are decidedly rare, but a few were collected by psychical researchers and found their way into the *Proceedings* of the Society for Psychical Research. They too serve to illustrate a small class of postmortem apparitions that rather forcefully suggest the persistence of some human beings after death.

Summing up the evidence for survival today

Does any of the evidence we have been discussing compel us to accept the survival theory? The answer is clearly no, since there remain those alternative theories that profess to explain the facts without assuming survival. To answer otherwise requires more positive evidence than we have that apparitions, mediumistic communicators, reincarnated egos and the like are really the persons they purport to be – i.e., that there is a provable, or at least inferable, continuity of consciousness between the communicating intelligence and some person who was once alive.

For this reason, parapsychologists traditionally look for cases in which the trance personalities or apparitions display blueprints of their identities, such as personal memories, characteristic intentions, habits, turns of phrase and general points of view. Much evidence fulfilling these requirements was collected by members of the SPR during the so-called golden age of mental mediumship (1890-1940) but those skeptical of survival rightly argued that even this evidence could not overcome the super-psi hypothesis. Always it remained possible that the apparition, trance personality or what have you, was not the living person but a simulacrum, a kind of lifelike puppet made to mouth lines scripted by the medium's ESP.

Many parapsychologists today, probably the majority, believe that an almost perfect stalemate exists between survivalist and non-survivalist interpretations of the evidence. Others, such as Osis, suggest that research efforts be continued and intensified in order to break down this impasse. These researchers, among them Stevenson, believe that special effort should be given to studying these categories of evidence that cannot readily be comprehended in terms of the super-ESP theory. Still other investigators have recommended various strategies that, if successful, would certainly cause trouble for the non-survival model. But none of these several proposals seems to be giving the proponents of the super-ESP theory many sleepless nights.

The most recent of these suggestions concerns cypher tests. First proposed by the late Robert Thouless of Cambridge University, the test requires the person wishing to communicate after death to graph out a cypher. Psychics would then be asked to break the code through ESP while its creator is still alive. If this proved impossible, the cypher-maker could then reveal the code after death through a medium or other suitable agency. Dr. Thouless felt that a successful communication of the code, under these conditions, could establish survival or at least make it more likely than not.

Since Thouless first made the suggestion, other parapsychologists have elaborated on it. Stevenson proposes the setting of a combination lock that can be opened through a verbal message translatable into digits. The person who prepares the lock could then, presuming he finds himself surviving death, communicate the verbal code through a medium.

Thouless prepared his own cypher before his death. J. G. Pratt, a close colleague of Stevenson's, left his friend a lock when he died a few years ago. So far, the cyphers have remained unbroken. But even if we assume a successful conclusion to the experiment, that does not mean that the researchers will have survived death. The medium, conceivably, could have picked up the key to the cypher from the investigator while he was still alive, then held the answer in reserve until such time as it could be used as a knockdown "test of survival." Nor are we obligated in the face of a successful cypher test to assume some paranormal explanation, since new inroads to computer technology now make it much easier to break even personal codes and cyphers by conventional means.

How we regard the evidence for survival is not in the last analysis, however, a function solely of the evidence. Like other great questions of life, our conclusion regarding survival depends in large measure on what William James, the famous psychologist and philosopher, called "our instinctive sense of the dramatic possibilities of nature."

If the combined sum of our experience and wisdom has taught us that the universe is not the kind of place where "spirits" may be said to exist, then naturally any other explanation for the phenomena will be preferable to survival. Even those who believe that the universe is far richer in realities than conventional science is willing or able to recognize may still balk at spirits on the grounds that everything else in nature seems to point sternly toward personal extinction.

But other persons, whose life experience has wrought a different conviction, may reasonably choose to accept the hypothesis of life after death as the readiest and least objectionable explanation for certain psychic phenomena. Survival, for them, accounts for the observed data while at the same time fitting their overall vision of the way the world is constituted.

The evidence, as it stands today, cannot definitively tell us whether or not we survive death. A rational case can be made for either view, whichever one we choose, depending upon our individual estimates of the "dramatic possibilities of nature." This personal factor will determine, to a greater or lesser degree, how each student of parapsychology regards the considerable evidence that has been collected.

FATE August and September 1986

AN INTERVIEW WITH DR. ELISABETH KÜBLER-ROSS
James Crenshaw

> *The boast of heraldry, the pomp of pow'r,*
> *And all that beauty, all that wealth e'er gave,*
> *Awaits alike th' inevitable hour:*
> *The paths of glory lead but to the grave.*
> — *Thomas Gray*
> *Elegy written in a country churchyard*

One the world's leading authorities on death and how to deal with it, Swiss-born psychiatrist Dr. Elisabeth Kübler-Ross, does not agree with 18th-century English poet Thomas Gray. On the basis of her observations and research she concludes that all paths lead beyond the grave.

In death she has found life; she says, "Death does not really exist. Death is simply a shedding of the physical body. And I do not just believe that. I know that. To me this is a very big difference."

Her conclusion is the result of her own independent findings – observations of many dying patients she has talked with before they crossed the border into "another reality." Often in their final words they reveal glimpses of that other reality and the expressions they use are remarkably similar when they describe how beautiful it is "over there"; how peaceful, how all pain has gone and how relatives and friends who have preceded them come to greet them.

Then there are the ones who "came back" – hundreds of reports she is now analyzing of persons who have "died" only to revive later and bring back detailed glimpses of the greater reality of a real world filled with life, color and beauty, so wonderful that most are reluctant to return.

Dr. Kübler-Ross also has been impressed by the number of "amazingly parallel" cases collected by other researchers, such as those Dr. Raymond A. Moody, Jr., a psychiatrist of Augusta, Georgia, published in his 1975 book *Life After Life*, and the 1892 article (translated from the German) by Albert Heim, a Zurich geologist, on near-fatal mountain climbing falls.

Heim found that most of the persons who fell, including himself, felt no grief or despair, no anxiety, but rather experienced a feeling of being "outside of time" in an eternal dimension of peace and beauty, sometimes with music.

Some revived drowning victims have related similar feelings of peace, beauty, a sense of happiness, occasional sounds of music and euphoric visions of vivid colors. Joel Guberman, a Toronto law student, reported these findings after making a study financed by the Canadian government.

Carl Jung also had a near-death experience after which he told of visions of beauty and a feeling of non-temporal ecstasy and tranquility so intense that he found it difficult to describe.

Dr. Elisabeth Kübler-Ross, a graduate of University of Zurich medical school, practices in Flossmoor, Illinois near Chicago.

Generally addressed as Dr. Ross, she has specialized in the problems of death and dying. She formerly was director of psychiatric and consultation services for hospitals of the University of Chicago.

What she has learned from the dying and those returned from death has profoundly affected her philosophy of living. In addition, she has had two dramatic experiences with the supposed dead which

Artist's concept of a temple in the afterlife. Credit: Raul daSilva.

have greatly influenced her life. One was the spontaneous appearance, seemingly in solid form, of a woman who had died.

This manifestation, while of a type known to psychic investigators, was extraordinary. Dr. Ross managed to induce the materialized figure to write a short note to a mutual friend.

Meanwhile, she had already begun to accumulate data from terminal patients who seemed to receive relatively consistent glimpses of another reality. They, too, in their final moments, usually were completely at peace, happy and without pain or fear. Also, in contrast with highly medicated patients or those with psychotic symptoms, their minds were clear, and they were capable of describing what they saw and heard.

These observations, as it turns out, are consistent with the returnees' statements. Here are some examples of both kinds from historical cases and other available literature. The first comments are from the dying:

> "It is beautiful!" were the last words of poetess Elizabeth Barrett Browning in 1861.

"It is very beautiful there" were the dying words of Thomas Edison in 1931.

"I didn't know it could be so beautiful!" a young American missionary said.

These are comments from people who have had an NDE:

An accident victim reported, "I floated farther and farther away."

"I seemed to be floating on a summer sea," a doctor said.

"The ego-consciousness, which was now me, seemed to be altogether outside my body, which I could see," said another doctor.

"I was floating in the air above my bed. I could see my body but had no interest in it," medium Arthur Ford said after an illness and two weeks in a coma.

"At first, I felt that my spirit, myself, was separating from the husk of my body and floating up to the ceiling of the room. From up there I could look down at my body on the operating table," reported an actor.

Shedding the physical body sometimes is experienced in connection with a tunnel:

"I seemed to float in a long tunnel. It appeared very narrow at first but gradually expanded into unlimited space," stated one woman who revived after "death."

"Then suddenly there appeared an opening like a tunnel and at the far end a light," reported an ill woman near death.

"I was floating in a long shaft that seemed very narrow at first and then became wider and wider," said a woman whose heart stopped for a time.

Others who had NDEs remarked on the peacefulness and lack of fear:

"You may think dying is unpleasant, but don't you believe it," said pilot Eddie Rickenbacker after a near-fatal air crash. "Dying is the sweetest, tenderest, most sensuous sensation I have ever experienced. Death comes disguised as a friend. All was serene; all was calm. How wonderful it would be simply to float out of this world. It is easy to die. You have to fight to live."

"There was no sense of pain, only a feeling of completeness and well-being," stated E. L. Huffine, airline captain, who survived "dying" in an early-day small plane crash.

"I was dead, and I saw them carry me into the house. I cannot describe the sensation of peace and happiness," reported a doctor who was thrown from a horse.

"I'll never be afraid of dying again… I was overcome by a feeling of deep content… I no longer felt any desire for earthly life," reported an elderly appendicitis patient.

"It was so peaceful and fine, and I felt ever so happy," one auto accident victim reported.

"My next sensation was of floating in a bright, pale yellow light – a very pleasant feeling," a revived cardiac patient said.

"I saw a sky over me that was bluer than anything I had ever seen on earth … and the higher I got the more the clouds turned violet. I heard music coming from far off," said another cardiac arrest patient.

"I saw a bright light in the distance… I heard sounds coming from this light… music with a curious harmony," reported a third cardiac case.

"While I was still unconscious, I felt myself floating in an atmosphere of peace and serenity… while in this beatific sphere, a local government officer I know quite well came forward to meet me… I did not know that this friend had passed on. I was told afterwards by my wife," reported a patient who revived after being in a coma.

"Frank, I didn't know you were there!" said a dying man who saw his mother, father, brother and sister who had predeceased him but who did not know his cousin Frank had died.

"I see the children's faces!" said a dying minister referring to two grandchildren who had predeceased him.

"Oh, it is lovely and bright!… I can see Father… he has Vida with him," was the vision of one terminal patient.

These brief excerpts are from cases cited in books published on this subject in the past: Dr. Robert Crookall's chapter "People Who Nearly Died" in his book *The Study and Practice of Astral Projection,* Jess E. Weiss' *The Vestibule,* Jean-Baptiste Delacour's *Glimpses of the Beyond,* John Myers' *Voices from the Edge of Eternity,* Norman Vincent Peale's *Stay Alive All Your Life* and Sir William Barrett's *Death-Bed Visions.*

Ironically, physicist Sir William Barrett's collection of deathbed observations (including those of his wife, Lady Florence Barrett, who was a physician and obstetrical surgeon) were published the year after his own death in 1925. As one of the organizers of the Society for Psychical Research in London in 1882, he had access to many such records and had gathered a series of typical cases over many years.

Both Sir William and Columbia University Professor James H. Hyslop – who helped reorganize the American Society for Psychical Research in 1906 and who also collected a number of cases of deathbed visions – were greatly impressed with the incidence of cases in which the patient appeared to see previously deceased persons, including many they did not know had died. Barrett includes an example of a man apparently dying in one country who seemed to "see" the apparitions of friends he did not know had died in England in his absence. He only confirmed their deaths after recovering and returning home to England.

In the light of this kind of historical background, it was inevitable that Dr. Ross, dealing as she does constantly with the problems of the dying, should encounter duplicate patterns, even though she was not familiar with much of the specific literature on the subject. In fact, as she undertook her own research she avoided reading much of the literature so that the data she accumulated would lead to independent conclusions and not be "contaminated" as she calls it.

Nevertheless, "common denominators" in the dying experience became evident, especially when she began to accumulate and receive hundreds of accounts from all over the world of patients who "died" and were resuscitated. These "common denominators" include:

> (1) In the last moments before clinical death the patient may report "a tremendous sense of peace and equanimity, without pain or discomfort. Most of my patients, when they die, have a fantastically peaceful expression on their faces."
>
> So beautiful was the experience of dying in so many cases that Dr. Ross feared this information might precipitate a wave of suicides. "And I didn't want to be responsible for that. Now further research has shown that suicide is not the answer. These people do not leave their problems behind them. They must face them again sooner or later, perhaps over and over again as part of the process of growth and learning." (Dr. Ross accepts the theory of reincarnation and is doing research in this area too.)
>
> (2) Dying patients are keenly aware of what is going on, as proved in the reports of those who later revive. "People are fully aware when they shake off the physical body. At an accident scene they may see their body lying there. In a hospital they may find themselves floating over the operating table, watching everything that goes on and listening to all the conversation. If there are any secrets passed around, they are secrets no longer.
>
> "We have received letters from (revived) patients who are upset because of derogatory statements made around them while they were out of their bodies. And people who have been in a coma for months and

months can tell you what went on and what happened to the staff or the family during this period," she stated.

(3) Those who "come back" are never again afraid to die. Many did not want to come back at all but were told by someone on the "other side" that it was not yet time for them to die. Others may have a tremendous urge to "let go" but may be impelled to return because of family or reasons of unfinished business. But they will never fear death again.

(4) Someone is always there on the "other side" to meet and welcome the dying person.

Dr. Ross emphasizes that the statements of dying patients and those who revive show remarkable clarity of mind. "These patients do not hallucinate. They are not psychotic or on drugs or have a high fever that may cause hallucinations. They have a high degree of perception and can, if they revive, describe in magnificent detail the attempts to resuscitate them."

She also says they often report a sense of wholeness in their out-of-body state. "A young patient who was blinded in a laboratory explosion could see perfectly. Another one who had lost a leg had two legs as he floated above his body." (He no doubt was experiencing what mediums often call the "astral body" or "etheric double." Dr. Robert Crookall, a British authority on out-of-body experiences, has found meaningful parallels between the statements of OBE subjects and communications through mediums. (His book, *The Study and Practice of Astral Projection*, mentioned previously, contains a series of such correlations.)

A number of the reports Dr. Ross has collected are from children who "died" and came back. "One child did not want to tell her mother how beautiful it was because mothers don't like to hear their children say they like some place better than home. Finally, the child told her father she had met her brother and described in detail how beautiful this meeting was. At the end she said, 'The only thing about it is, I never had a brother.' At this point her father began to cry and told her that she had indeed had a brother who had died three months before she was born."

Children often encounter religious figures under such circumstances, depending upon their religious background. When Dr.

Ross asks these dying children whom they would like to have with them all the time, they almost all say "Mommy" or "Daddy."

"Yet not one of these children has seen 'Mommy' or 'Daddy' at the time of transition if the parents are still alive. They may see grandparents or other relatives who have gone on or one of these religious figures. The common denominator here is love. They do not see anyone who has been the subject of turmoil or bitterness."

Once Dr. Ross was approached by a mother who was deeply concerned over what her two-year-old son had said when he literally came back from the dead. On being revived the child said he had been in a most beautiful place where he saw Jesus and Mary. He did not want to leave but Mary told him the time for him to stay was not right and that he had to go back "to save your Mommy from the fire."

For 11 years the mother had worried about this experience, afraid to tell anyone, and feeling sad and depressed because this implied she was a sinner and it was up to her child to save her. Dr. Ross assured her this was not the correct interpretation of the little boy's imagery.

Suddenly, as the mother relived the memories of the child's death she realized what it would have been like if he had not returned. Dr. Ross said, "She grabbed her head and cried, 'Oh, my God! I would have gone through hell and fire!'"

Noted parapsychologist Dr. Karlis Osis has dealt with dying persons' visions of religious figures both in a pilot study of "Deathbed Observations by Physicians and Nurses" for the Parapsychology Foundation of New York (published in 1961) and in continued studies in this country and India for the American Society for Psychical Research.

Taking into account a multiplicity of variables and elaborate computer analyses based on answers to questionnaires, he indicates that the religious "hallucinations" represent a kind of subjective imagery. Yet he finds that the data as a whole indicate some form of "external activity" that transcends purely subjective experience; particularly apparitions of relatives and friends, which he refers to as "takeaway" visions of the deceased, may have objectivity.

"Reality we all see is approximately the same," he says, "but fantasies differ with each individual and each nation."

He found a highly significant consistency in the reports of deathbed visions both in the United States and India, including the descriptions of beauty, harmony and peace, as well as welcoming friends and relatives. "We found the same core phenomena in the experiences of the dying in both cultures," he says, but "the embroidery is different."

He also seeks to distinguish symbols of inner conflicts, hopes, desires, expectations, memories, rambling and confused hallucinations based on this world concerns from glimpses of another reality, a reality with a purpose.

"This 'afterlife purpose' emerges like a peak above the clouds and dominates the findings," he declares. For instance, the purpose of the "takeaway" apparitions seems dearly to escort the dying patient to another existence, another reality. On the other hand, the rambling kind of hallucinations have no apparent purpose.

The reality and universal nature of the "takeaway" phenomenon were commented on by Dr. Norman Vincent Peale in his book *The Power of Positive Thinking*. He said it "recurs again and again in the incidents which have come to my attention… So repetitive is this phenomenon and so similar are the characteristics of this experience as described by many that it amounts to a substantial evidence that the people whose names are called, whose faces are seen, are actually present."

Elisabeth Kübler-Ross agrees but her research is not confined to statements of dying patients. Two personal experiences have spurred her into many new directions of inquiry. First, a medium who did not know her told Dr. Ross something she did not know – that her mother had died. This was confirmed later in the day by a message from Switzerland where her mother had been hospitalized for four years, paralyzed because of a stroke.

As the medium proceeded to make some general statements about the mother, Dr. Ross, very skeptical, decided to ask a mental question: "Was there anything else I could have done for you?"

The answer came through the medium instantly, "Yes, you never asked me if I had a headache. It would have been such a relief if somebody had given me something for my headache. And I'm not telling you this to make you feel guilty but to make you a better physician."

Dr. Ross explains that her mother was unable to speak for four years and able to communicate only by blinking her eyes during the earlier stages of the paralysis. As a result of this message, Dr. Ross asked many people who work with stroke patients if they ever give anything for headaches. One physician replied in annoyance that it was "totally impossible" for such a patient to have a headache. Dr. Ross exploded, "Listen, if my mother said she had a headache, she had a headache!"

The case of Mrs. S. caused Dr. Ross to embark on a full investigation of the experiences of those who have "died" and revived. Mrs. S., a woman in her 50s, was a longtime victim of Hodgkin's disease. She attended one of the Kübler-Ross seminars and shared her experience of "dying." She had found herself floating above her body, watching the medical team trying to resuscitate her. She saw them give up, pull a sheet over her and wheel her away to the hospital morgue. Then she "came back," managed to push the sheet away from her face and was returned to the hospital ward.

She asked Dr. Ross if this indicated she was psychotic. The doctor assured her it did not. It was learned later that Mrs. S. did finally die.

Subsequently (in 1968) Dr. Ross was about to make an important decision. She felt that she could not continue her work with terminal patients and was on the point of making her decision known when Mrs. S. appeared to her – not as an apparition but as a solid, three-dimensional, living human being.

"I was in the corridor of the hospital near the elevator when Mrs. S. appeared. I was about to tell a minister friend about my decision, but she interrupted me in front of the elevator and he went on down to the street level. She asked if she could see me for a few minutes. So, we walked into my office and she leaned over my desk and told me she had come for only two reasons; one was to thank us. The second was that she wanted me to promise her that the work would continue. I promised."

Then Dr. Ross resorted to "a little white lie." She needed some proof that Mrs. S. was actually there.

"You see, I was totally shocked and in those days I didn't believe in anything like this. I told her a colleague who had been a partner with me in the seminar would like to have a note from her.

"I knew instantly that she knew why I asked for that. But with a knowing smile on her face she wrote a short greeting to my friend and afterward walked out of the office."

Although Dr. Ross's experience was unusual, I assured her there have been many reported cases of spontaneous materializations, including innumerable accounts of so-called "phantom hitchhikers" who hail a driver, are given a lift, then disappear and later are found to be deceased. In many instances long ordinary conversations take place with the "living ghost."

There also have been numerous cases of ghost writing, in which even a name and address was written on a card and the writing later identified by family members.

However, Dr. Ross's experience is possibly the first case on record in which an apparently solid spirit figure, appearing spontaneously, has been induced to give a handwriting sample.

As a result of the encounter, Dr. Ross and her colleagues have continued their research. She refers to herself as "a middle-aged physician who has become well known throughout the country as 'The Dead and Dying Lady.'" But to thousands of troubled souls, present and departed, she is a beautiful and tender link between two realities, the here and the hereafter – that other reality her patients have helped her to discover.

In her book *Death: The Final Stage of Growth* she puts it this way, "This work with dying patients has helped me to find my own religious identity, to know that there is life after death and to know that we will be reborn again one day in order to complete the tasks we have not been able or willing to complete in this lifetime. It is in this context that I also begin to see the meaning of suffering and understand why even children have to die."

[Elisabeth Kübler-Ross: 1926-2004.]

FATE April 1977

THE PSYCHIC WORLD OF DYING CHILDREN
D. Scott Rogo

Dr. Elizabeth Kübler-Ross is best known for her psychological work with dying patients. Her first book on the subject, *On Death and Dying,* was published in 1969 and became a bestseller. Her primary discovery was that people exhibit four stages or reactions before finally accepting death. They usually first deny the fact, then display anger toward their fate, try to bargain with God for more time and finally enter into a deep state of depression. Once they survive this dark night of the soul, they emerge prepared to face life's final journey.

      Whether these stages of dying are predictable and sequential reactions to terminal illness, or whether they really even exist, is still being debated by psychologists. But by bringing her experiences before the general public, Dr. Kübler-Ross gave society a new appreciation of the complexities of death. She took the subject out of the closet and made it a topic for discussion.

This pioneering physician followed her seminal studies with a sequel entitled *Questions and Answers on Death and Dying* in 1974. Seven years later her *Living With Death and Dying* was published. This book represented a significant change in Dr. Kübler-Ross's thinking and research.

The Swiss-born psychiatrist previously had been concerned primarily with people coming to the end of long and productive lives. But in *Living With Death and Dying* she devoted a significant chapter to the care of dying children. In the late 1970s Kübler-Ross became fascinated with the challenge of counseling these young patients. She specialized in their psychological care, and her book *On Children and Death* explores the psychological world of the dying child. Surprisingly, the book doesn't concern merely the psychological aspects of this inner world but also deals with the dying child's psychic perceptions and experiences.

Parapsychologists have known for a long time that some people become extremely psychic when faced with death. Children are not an exception. Perhaps the first researcher to bring widespread attention to this fact was Sir William Barrett, a Dublin physicist and cofounder (in 1882) of the Society for Psychical Research in Great Britain. In his posthumously published and celebrated book *Death-Bed Visions* the researcher cites an unusual incident reported from the United States.

The story concerned two small children who were dying of diphtheria, then a serious bacterial disease usually resulting in death. Jennie and Edith were close friends, and both contracted the disease in June 1889. Jennie died first but little Edith's parents and physicians took pains to keep the information from their charge. Three days following the first child's death, however, Edith reported a welcoming figure at her bedside. She instantly realized she was dying and suddenly stared toward the invisible presence in the room.

"Why, Papa, I am going to take Jennie with me!" she exclaimed. "Why, Papa, you did not tell me that Jennie was here!" She then reached toward the phantom and said, "Oh, Jennie, I'm so glad you are here." She died soon after saying these words to her surprised parents.

Cases of such deathbed visions could be dismissed if they weren't so commonly reported. A serious and detailed study of similar deathbed phenomena was undertaken by Professor James H. Hyslop who republished his results in his book *Psychical Research and the*

Resurrection in 1908. (Hyslop began his career teaching philosophy at Columbia University and later, in 1907, helped found the American Society for Psychical Research.)

While engaged in his research, he uncovered a curious book published by the parents of Daisy Dryden, a little girl who had died in Marysville, California on September 9, 1854. Some sort of progressive enteritis caused her death and she expired four days after falling ill. During those critical days she became so clairvoyant that her mother constantly sat by her side taking copious notes. The little patient reported seeing a series of "spirit" visitors at her bedside. Often these figures claimed to be her deceased relatives, but Daisy also perceived deceased friends and relatives of her neighbors and delivered evidential messages from them.

Similar stories were commonly reported when child mortality was still high in this country and when most persons died in their own homes, surrounded by friends and relatives. Death has been progressively robbed of its spiritual essence by the mechanization of society; today patients rarely return home to die. Instead they die in their hospital rooms, often sedated and unconscious and hooked up to life support systems.

Kübler-Ross refuses to champion this impersonal approach to death and the lack of regard for the dying. She prefers to counsel the dying wherever they remain most comfortable and through this practice she has gradually rediscovered the psychic world of dying children. Children seem intuitively conscious of death and sense its presence whether it comes from disease or sudden accident. Kübler-Ross reports on their experiences in her book *On Children and Death*.

"One couple shared the story of their little eight-year-old girl who died by a freak accident during a trip overseas," the psychiatrist reports, "and how they missed the cues that they might have been better off not going on the trip at all."

When the little girl fell and struck her head, her parents rushed her to a hospital, but the facility was several miles away and the child survived for only 20 minutes. Later the parents realized that their daughter had intuited her death. Even on the overseas flight, the child wrote a thank-you note to the family's (future) hosts. She had never written such a note before. She then gave the letter to her sister, asking that she deliver it. She seemed to realize she wouldn't live to deliver the letter personally.

Remarkable, too, is a letter Kübler-Ross received from a similarly distraught parent. Two days before her daughter was killed in a traffic mishap, the correspondent took the girl to dinner. During the meal they discussed their future and the girl's mother expressed some concern over her daughter's declining school grades. That's when the girl said suddenly that it simply didn't matter. "My life is almost over," she told her startled mother.

The way the girl obviously prepared for her upcoming death was even more bizarre. "She spent the last couple of days ironing everything," the mother wrote in her letter to Kübler-Ross. "This is a 15-year-old child, you know. I was just amazed. And she didn't take any identification with her [the day of the accident] and so I see it as an act of love because she knew. She knew when she left to go in the car that she would not be coming home again; she didn't want me to be awakened at 1:30 in the morning to be told that my daughter had died. I didn't find out until three the next day."

These comments become clearer when the entire letter is read. The child always took her ID card with her when she left the house, so this singular oversight was significant, in the mother's opinion. The girl left the ID at her bedside right next to her diary and when the mother explored further she found an important message inscribed in the book. The message was written for her mother's benefit and it exhorted her to self-heal the pain she felt. The girl obviously expected her mother to find the passage.

Kübler-Ross cites additional cases of children suddenly beginning to talk about death, reincarnation and other spiritual issues just before life-threatening accidents. These cases do not always represent simple precognitions or intuitions of death, however. Sometimes the children actually received some kind of spiritual revelation. The most sensational letter the psychiatrist received came from a parent on the East Coast and fits directly into this category. This mother related that her daughter woke up early one morning extremely euphoric and excited. She had slept in her mother's bed that night and woke her sleepy parent by spontaneously shaking and hugging her.

"Mom, Mom!" she kept saying, "Jesus told me I'm going to heaven! I enjoy to go to heaven [sic], Mama, and it's all beautiful and gold and silver and shiny, and Jesus and God are there."

The girl was talking so fast and frantically that her mother couldn't remember all she said.

"[Her speech] was affected mostly by her excitement," the correspondent wrote to Kübler-Ross. "[My daughter] was by nature a calm, almost contemplative child, extremely intelligent, but not much given to the wildness and bounding-about-silliness that many four-year-olds get. She was verbally skilled and very precise with her speech. To find her so excited that she was stammering and tripping over her words was very unusual. In fact, I don't remember ever seeing her in such a state, not at Christmas, birthdays or the circus."

The mother tried to calm the child, but the little girl's enthusiasm couldn't be squelched. She kept talking of the angels, the jewels she saw in heaven and the beings she would meet there. Finally, almost in despair, the child's mother tried to reason with her.

"If you went to heaven, I'd miss you," she said. "And I'm glad you had such a happy dream, but let's slow down and relax a minute, okay?"

But the girl kept talking about her experience. "It was not a dream," she insisted. "It was real." She emphasized her claim in that dejected way little children sometimes have when protesting. She said further that she would care for her mother from heaven. This conversation continued for several minutes before the child finally relented and went out to play. Sometime later in the afternoon the girl was found murdered. Her life came to its tragic end seven hours after she received the revelation.

Many people will find the subject of dying children and their psychic world depressing. We usually feel bitterness when a child's life is suddenly cut short either by accident or by childhood disease such as leukemia. But Kübler-Ross presents a spiritually uplifting side of this dark picture. Her cases indicate that some power prepared these children for death and they seemed intent on sharing this information with their parents. In fact, the process of sharing seems to be a consistent feature of such cases.

Because I personally believe in life after death, I do not feel too bitter when a child dies. My feelings are based on cases similar to Kübler-Ross's which already are part of parapsychology's rich literature.

In the last case related by Kübler-Ross, for instance, although there can be no doubt that the murder was tragic and senseless, the child openly welcomed her death and looked forward to her future life in heaven.

This brings us to Kübler-Ross's second important finding on children and death. The psychological process of dying can be spiritually uplifting, and the psychiatrist has collected several cases reminiscent of previously published reports by Dr. William Barrett and Professor James Hyslop.

Kübler-Ross is primarily concerned with helping dying children accept and deal with life's end. But sometimes she finds her work hampered by the family's primary care physician. Doctors remain reluctant to tell their patients the sad truth concerning their terminal illnesses. Because of their perhaps understandable bias, sometimes they have refused to let Kübler-Ross work with the patients in a completely open fashion. She feels that these children intuitively know when they're dying, however, and don't really need to be told. The dedicated psychiatrist has stayed at the bedside of these young patients sometimes to the end of their short lives. What she has experienced could serve as a lesson to the medical profession in general.

"Shortly before children die there is often a very 'clear moment,' as I call it," writes Kübler-Ross in *On Children and Death*. "Those who have remained in a coma since [their] accident or surgery open their eyes and seem very coherent. Those who have had great pain and discomfort are very quiet and at peace. It is in these moments that I asked them if they were willing to share with me what they were experiencing."

The results of these inquiries eventually contributed to Kübler-Ross's personal belief in spiritual immortality. The psychiatrist was summoned during one such crisis to the bedside of a traffic accident victim. The boy's mother had been killed in the fiery crash, but his brother Peter survived and was being treated in a different hospital where the facilities included a better burn center. When the psychiatrist asked her charge whether he felt okay, the boy replied with a surprising comment.

"Yes, everything is all right now," he told Kübler-Ross. "Mommy and Peter are already waiting for me." The little boy smiled contentedly and slipped back into a coma from which he failed to recover.

"I was quite aware that his mother had died at the scene of the accident, but Peter had not died," the veteran counselor reports. "He had been brought to a special burn unit in another hospital severely burnt, because the car caught fire before he was extricated from the wreck. Since I was only collecting data, I accepted the boy's information and determined to look in on Peter. It was not necessary however, because as I passed the nursing station there was a call from the other hospital to inform me that Peter had died a few minutes earlier."

Psychologists know that shortly before dying, terminal patients often see figures coming to welcome them. The widespread incidence of this phenomenon was first formally documented in 1961 when Dr. Karlis Osis, then a researcher with the New York-based Parapsychology Foundation, published his monograph *Deathbed Observations by Physicians and Nurses*. This study reported the results of a survey of 5,000 physicians and 5,000 nurses in this country. Those healthcare professionals who responded to the survey reported that their dying patients commonly claimed to see either beautiful landscapes or phantom visitors in their sickrooms. The apparitions usually represented spirits of the dead or were interpreted to be religious figures such as messengers from heaven.

After Osis became research director for the American Society for Psychical Research (also in New York), he expanded his research. He wished to compare deathbed experiences from this culture with those from a foreign society. So, the Latvian-born psychologist conducted surveys among physicians and health care professionals in this country and in India. His results prove that deathbed reports in the United States and India are similar. Since few of the patients were taking drugs when their visions occurred, Osis and his collaborators believe that their data point directly to survival of death.

Despite this research, some psychologists and parapsychologists still remain skeptical of Osis's conclusions. While deathbed visions and revelations probably are not a result of brain dysfunction (such as progressive oxygen starvation), the possibility remains that these experiences represent a curious form of psychological phenomena. Some skeptics suggest that the brain artificially produces the experiences to reduce the patient's fear of death. Such visions may reconcile the dying patient to his fate and help him accept his own mortality. For this reason, evidential cases such as those reported by Kübler-Ross become important. They indicate that the patient is experiencing a real visitation, an experience that conventional psychology cannot explain away.

In her book the psychiatrist writes, "In all the years that I have quietly collected data from California to Sydney, Australia, from white and black children, aboriginals, Eskimos, South Americans and Libyan youngsters, every single child who mentioned that someone was waiting for [him] mentioned a person who had actually preceded [him] in death, even if by only a few moments. And yet none of these children had been informed of the recent death of the relative by us at any time. Coincidence? By now there is no scientist or statistician who could convince me that this occurs, as some colleagues claim, as 'a result of oxygen deprivation' or for other 'rational and scientific' reasons."

Because these cases present such impressive evidence, Kübler-Ross believes in a life after death. She couples the importance of deathbed visions with the many near-death experience (NDE) reports she has collected from her patients from people who journeyed into the next world during close brushes with death. This emphasis on the spiritual dimensions of the death experience is reflected in Kübler-Ross's thinking in a third important way. She collects and publishes purported cases of children who returned from death to comfort their grieving parents.

In her book, for instance, she writes about a mother who was feeling total despair. Her six-year-old daughter had been sexually assaulted and killed and the incident had struck fear into the heart of the small community in which she lived. A few days after the death, the mother was resting in her bedroom when a bright light suddenly shone through the window. Within this light her child appeared, smiling radiantly. The figure disappeared within a few moments, but the vision greatly comforted the mother.

"The sight filled her with such peace and love," writes Kübler-Ross, "that she was in a much better mental condition after this incident than the rest of the still-frightened community!"

Kübler-Ross continues to explore the private worlds of dying children. She is expanding her work to include the spiritual, psychic and psychological issues involved. Probably her best advice, repeated in each of her books, is that society learn to live with death. Perhaps we can learn to appreciate death as a final chance for ultimate personal growth. The courage and spiritual fulfillment so many children have found during the process of dying should represent an important lesson for us. Their experiences don't reflect the fears so many of us feel when we face the subject of death. Kübler-Ross has redirected us to a wise and ancient truth, first pointed out in the Bible: When it comes to spiritual matters, little children can be our best teachers.

[Elisabeth Kübler-Ross: 1926-2004.]

D. Scott Rogo (1950-1990): Prolific writer and author on paranormal and afterlife topics; FATE columnist.

FATE September 1987

LET MY BROTHER GO
Patti Paster

My brother Gene McVicker, [a pseudonym], the oldest of five children, loved his family, he loved his friends and he loved his country. Many years ago, in Brooklyn, New York, I beamed with pride as I watched my big brother graduate from St. Gregory's Parochial, St. Francis Prep and Brooklyn College with the highest scholarly honors. "Genie the Brain," as we lovingly called him, was indeed a hard act to follow.

He married a wonderful woman named Alice and together they raised three beautiful and caring children. It was the quality of his life that counted, not the short number of years allotted him.

His heart's greatest desire was to please his beloved dad by proving he could win in the game of life by playing fair. The desire was never fully realized because Dad passed away at the age of 54, never to see his firstborn son become an outstanding overseas representative of the United States government.

Sadly, my younger sister, Terry, was unable to witness his "winning" either because she died of cancer in 1969, when she was only 29 years old.

In the quiet, early morning hours of November 19, 1985, my sister appeared to me in a dream. Never had I seen her look so beautiful and peaceful. She never uttered a word but her angelic, loving smile told me she was coming back to help one of her family pass through the door of death and into the light of the land hereafter.

When I woke up, I was experiencing intense pressure in the northwest section of my body. If it had been on the other side of my chest, I would have sworn I was having a heart attack. Suddenly I knew what the dream meant. I knew for whom she was coming. My brother, on sick leave from his office in the Philippines, was living with his family in Seattle, Washington, the northwest section of the United States.

On Thanksgiving evening, exactly nine days after my dream, Gene, 49, had his first seizure and was taken by the paramedics to the University Hospital in Seattle. At noon the following Wednesday I flew up from Los Angeles so that I could minister to him in the only way I knew, by sharing my love and prayers.

At one point in the course of the many conversations Alice and I had that week, I delicately mentioned my dream about Terry. Alice was quite interested. She said that it explained something that had been puzzling her.

Every night, she told me, she would sleep next to Gene's bed on a small cot the hospital had supplied. In the last few evenings she had awakened to the sound of Gene's voice. He was sitting up in bed talking to his sister Terry and reaching out as if he were touching her.

On Monday, December 9, 1985, exactly 20 months to the very date of my sister's death – and, coincidentally, the expiration date printed on his US passport – my brother announced to his wife, "Alice, I'm getting out of here."

"That's right, Gene," she said. "We're taking you home on Friday."

But the home Gene was referring to was not the same one Alice was talking about.

Around 9:30 that morning Alice and I decided to go downstairs for breakfast since Gene's favorite blonde nurse was going to give him a sponge bath and replace the bedding. Alice told him where we were going and kidded him about not fooling around with the nurse while we were gone. He laughed the same hearty laugh that I loved to hear.

Poor Alice. She was so mentally and physically drained by this ordeal that I suggested she go home after breakfast and try to get some uninterrupted sleep. I told her I would stay by my brother's side that day.

"Okay, Patti, you win," she said. "You're right. I'm so exhausted I can't even think anymore. I'll go back, kiss him good-bye and go home for the day."

On our return from the cafeteria we passed the nurse's station and asked how everything was going. Gene's nurse told us that all went well and after his sponge bath he fell asleep. She added that, while she was bathing him, he kept talking to "someone named Terry."

When Alice and I entered his room, we sensed immediately that something was wrong. He did not respond to our greetings in his usual cheerful manner. He seemed to be in another world, looking out into space. Alice ran quickly to get the doctor.

After examining him, the doctor started giving instructions to the nurse and before we knew it, six or seven doctors and nurses were crowding around Gene's bed. Because Alice could not bear to watch them put even one more injection into her beloved husband's arms, already black and blue from numerous needle bruises, we stepped aside and waited at the door.

A few minutes later a nurse rushed past us with the medical equipment that would revive my brother's heart whenever it stopped beating.

Alice, in a state of shock, couldn't believe what was happening. Gene was supposed to have two more months to live. The children had already bought him Christmas gifts. He was coming home on Friday!

I put my arms around Alice. "Gene would never choose to be artificially alive," I said to her. "I beg you, Alice, please let my brother go. Please, please let him get off his cross of cancer."

With that Alice shook her head no to the use of that "torture machine" – the machine that revived him so that he could endure further agony.

Doing our best to stop our tears, we went to Gene's bedside. He was still breathing on his own and his eyes were still gazing out into space. Alice placed her tape recorder on Gene's pillow so that he could hear his favorite classical music. She lovingly held his left hand and kept telling him how much she and the rest of the family loved him and how proud they were to have shared his love and his life.

I stood at his right side and held his other hand close to my heart. Then I gently placed my right hand over his heart and prayed softly.

Then my brother died. Through the tears that were clouding my physical vision. I saw my father reaching out with his hands to receive my brother, preparing to welcome him home.

FATE December 1986

SUFFERING DURING THE DYING PROCESS HAS A PURPOSE
Rebecca Conroy-Costello

As a psychic medium and medical intuitive, I get asked all kinds of interesting questions. But one in particular always stands out for me: "Why did my loved one struggle so much when they were dying?"

I have also asked myself that same question on more than one occasion. As a registered nurse, my specialty was end of life care. I also had a very close friend in his 40s who was going through the worst case of cancer suffering I had ever seen. What started out as leukemia wound up a very invasive and disfiguring head and neck cancer.

I had never seen a human endure what he had – the surgeries, the pain – a former Marine was made into what felt like a "wooden man" due to a bad case of Graft vs. Host disease. His death literally went on for years. The things he endured because of his fear of death were mind-boggling. I frequently asked myself, Why is he not letting go? Even when he called me a few months before his passing and asked me to help him as he was finally ready to transition in the next life, he was upset that his body just wouldn't let go. He asked me why he was still here.

In my line of work, I am used to doing psychic detective work to find answers for my clients. I researched this for him. I was surprised at the answer. This was his way of burning of karma for the shenanigans of his younger years and the pain he caused others.

In the years of my doing this end of life care, I found there seem to be common threads to suffering during the dying processes.

The reasons for this will make little sense to you, and it feels cruel to live out the last days of life this way. However, the soul doesn't care about our human perceptions. On some level, we create all that happens to us and the soul simply accepts these as lessons. It is a person's soul who makes the choice on how to leave this world, not our conscious mind. Our souls and spirit perceive the lessons as valuable and necessary for spiritual advancement. Our humanness says this is merciless. I assure you, the soul never suffered. It was in a "different classroom."

Living a good life of kindness and selflessness doesn't necessarily mean that passing will be effortless. Some souls experience a slower dying process because of fear of crossing over.

Perhaps they feel they were bad people and will be "punished" by their God. Perhaps they are plagued with guilt and doubtful there is life beyond the human existence they have known.

Sometimes things are long and drawn out and painful before entering the higher vibrations of light. The soul chose this as a way to leave behind and dissolve emotional, mental, spiritual and physical blocks and accumulated energy that may prevent him or her from rising to higher levels of light upon passing from this world into the next.

Sometimes, a person may choose the slower experience of dying to become more aware of their divine self. It is only the physical and ego self that suffers. Dying pushes your soul to the forefront whether or not you're ready. The soul understands its journey, the choices it makes to heal, to uncover the truth, and to discover its own divinity.

Other times, people linger and die slowly as a way of bringing comfort to those they will leave behind. It can be hard to let go. Sometimes a bit of additional time can allow the family to prepare or stage the grief in smaller intervals. Loved ones may want to hold on and cannot imagine life without them. It gives the family time to let go and say all that they need to say.

It is also possible there was hurt between the dying person and a loved one. A slower dying process can be an opportunity to review one's life. The person may undergo a slower passing as a way to allow the hurt to heal between them and to find forgiveness.

There are also some warrior souls who choose to suffer to lift the burdens and pain of others. Conscious suffering can lift the suffering and burdens of others when it encompasses and transmutes pain that is bigger than the individual. Envision that your loved one's pain was lessening the pain of children who were suffering. They are healing pain in others who cannot do it for themselves. It's a way for them to add light into the global consciousness. One last act of love.

We need our suffering to have meaning even if we do not understand it from a human perspective. Sometimes suffering is more than physical pain. Confusion and loneliness can settle in when life seems to have little purpose. What they go through and what their family and friends go through is not without purpose. It provides the fertile ground from which your soul grows and develops deeper meaning.

Please know that we are never alone.

This includes your dying loved one. Many people become aware during the process of dying that there is life after death. They learn this as they begin to see their loved ones on the Other Side and when making frequent trips into the Spirit realm to get their new home ready before they cross over. When they do leave this world, they have not left you. They have just changed form. They will still communicate messages to you on a regular basis. They are aware of things in your life even after they have left this place. When they leave, they have no pain, no anger or sorrow. Those denser emotions drop away. Heaven is merely a window away... you just have to open the curtains.

Rebecca Conroy-Costello: Registered nurse, psychic medium, medical intuitive, Reiki Master and spiritual counselor.

FATE #729

WHY THE CHRISTIAN CHURCH MUST STUDY SURVIVAL
Reverend Robert E. Allen

It all began on a hot summer afternoon in 1952. I had just served the sacrament of Holy Communion to Mr. Thurston Wiggin of East Corinth, Maine, who was dying of leukemia. I had made frequent visits to the Wiggins' home to bring peace of heart and mind to this valiant man.

As the months wore on, however, the dying man came to realize that his was a losing battle. Finally, he requested that I bring the Lord's Supper to his bedside so that he could experience one last hour of fellowship with Christ. After he had received the bread and the wine he closed his eyes; his head sank back onto the pillow and he breathed a sigh of relief. His face seemed to be more relaxed and peaceful than I remembered seeing it in all the time I had been ministering to him. I knew he had made his peace with God.

As I rose to leave the sickroom Mr. Wiggin turned his head toward me, opened his eyes, and said in a weak voice, "I don't suppose I'll be here much longer. My loved ones on the other side were all here last night. They waved to me and said, 'Thurston, you'll be seeing us again soon. We are coming to take you home. Helen also will be joining us before too long.'"

Fortunately, his wife, Helen, was out of the room and did not hear the last part of his statement. I quickly leaned over the bed and said to him, "We hope that you were only dreaming. You'll be around for quite a while yet, so don't take this experience too seriously."

Young pastors, in their zeal to bring immediate comfort, sometimes make brash statements; this was one of my most regrettable false messages of hope. I shall never forget its resultant effect.

A strange look came over Mr. Wiggin's face as he struggled to frame the words, "It was no dream, Pastor Allen, I was wide awake at the time. I saw those people and they were as real as you are. Don't you believe in angels and life beyond the grave?"

I hastily assured him that I did believe in life eternal and then sputtered something about remembering him in my prayers. I made a rapid exit.

As I drove back to the parsonage I thought to myself how unfortunate it was that opiates had been used in such quantities to deaden physical pain that the mind became delirious and thought processes distorted.

Less than a week later I committed Thurston Wiggin's physical body to our "Holy Mother, The Earth" in a simple ceremony. His wife, Helen, wept quietly as I intoned the final words of the benediction. She left the grave with the words, "I'm glad that his suffering is over and that he is now at home with the Lord."

"Yes," 1 thought to myself, "had he lived on too much longer he might have lost his mind completely; it would have been a horrible thing. As it was he died quietly with full confidence in a beautiful illusion."

I called on Helen Wiggin two or three times after that. She seemed to be adjusting to her new life. Her grief was intense, but she showed every indication of being able to conquer it in the due course of time. She was in good health, had a nice family of grown children and was qualified to teach school and thus earn a comfortable living.

Two years later Helen Wiggin died on the operating table, during a routine surgical operation from which everyone had expected

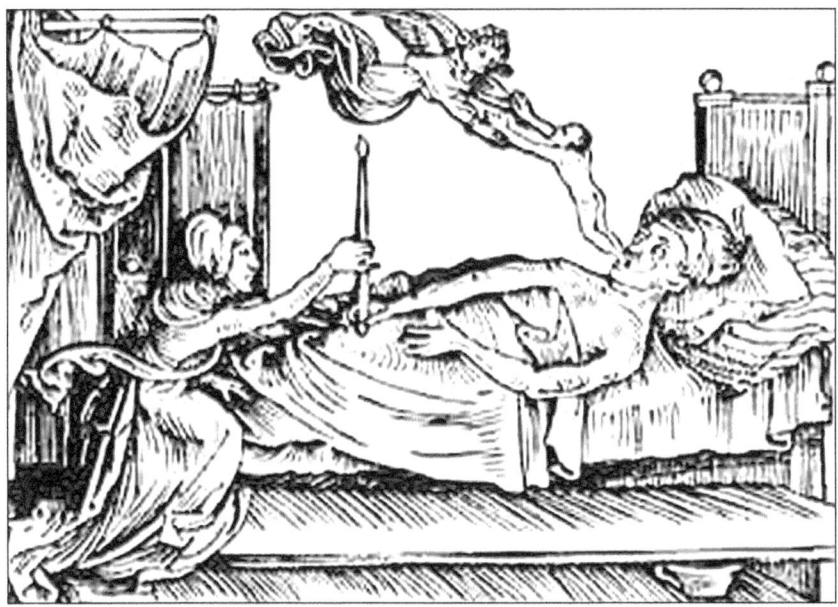

An angel receives the soul of a dying man. Credit: Wikimedia Commons.

her to recover. I was stunned when I was informed of her passing. The prophetic words of her dead husband's revelators had come true.

"Helen will be joining us soon," they had said.

Her untimely death seemed to me more than a coincidence.

I decided I had better talk this matter of immortality over with a more seasoned minister. I had just registered as a graduate student at Harvard Divinity School and I felt that the most likely consultant would be one of the seminary professors there. I made an appointment to talk with one of them.

He advised me not to be disturbed about this experience. "There is a life beyond the grave," he said, "but you and I cannot dogmatize concerning its exact nature. We must accept its existence by faith. If we trust in God He will lead us into the fuller understanding of it when our turn comes to make the journey beyond the veil of mystery. The Bible discourages any undue probing into this mystical realm but it is safe to assume that there have been occasions on which the dead have returned momentarily to warn of impending crisis or the imminence of death for a loved one. Don't forget," he counseled, "we do believe in the Communion of Saints."

When I returned to Maine I visited an experienced Baptist minister. This good brother was greatly disturbed when I told him of my professor's statement.

"Don't be misled by that modernist, Bob," he shouted. "The scriptures clearly teach that the dead are in a state of unconsciousness until the day of Christ's return. Then, and only then, will they become alive again. The righteous dead will at that time reign in heaven with the Lord; the wicked sinners will be relegated to Hell. The dead do not return to this life as we know it."

He pounded his desk to emphasize the finality of what he was saying.

I was so impressed with this demonstration of zeal that I decided to begin a comprehensive study of the Bible's teaching concerning life beyond this dimension of existence. I decided that if the scriptures supported his point of view I would probe no further.

I found, to my amazement, that the Bible does not set forth one unified point of view. It speaks against the practice of communion with familiar or ancestral spirits for the sake of auguring the future, but it also seems to look with favor upon those who presumably wrestled with angels and upon those who entertained angelic or spirit messengers.

The Book of Ecclesiastes does not seem to be compatible with any theory of life beyond the grave. The New Testament speaks of the validity of the concept of the spiritual resurrection; it also exhorts its readers to test the spirits to see if they are of God – the inference being that some are of God and some are of the devil.

I concluded that even the inspired writers of the scripture tended to interpret their beliefs toward personal, conscious survival after death in the light of the religious customs of their day and in the context of their own personal experience.

I also decided that many ministers merely use this sacred book as they would employ the Rorschach test – it becomes an instrument into which they project their own theological opinions. They simply read their own views into the scripture for the purpose of rationalizing or sanctifying them.

The weight of evidence from the Bible, however, seems to be in favor of personal conscious survival after death and the probable access of discarnate personalities who survive the change called death.

I went from one sincere minister to another in an effort to find out just what the consensus of trained, experienced ministerial opinion was. I found no uniform pattern to guide my thinking. My ideas concerning life after death now were completely confused. I was tempted to drop the whole matter once and for all. I knew that death would come to me someday and then I would have the only verifiable answer.

I was returning by train from Harvard to my student parish at Oakland, Maine. A stranger took the seat next to mine. I was busily engaged in reading *You Will Survive After Death* by Sherwood Eddy. I noticed the man seemed very interested in my book.

"What do you think of the book?" he finally asked.

"I find it very interesting," I replied, "but as far as I can see it is just another attempt to prove something which cannot be verified so long as we are dwellers on this finite plane of existence."

The man gave me a strange look and replied, "I think that this matter of life after death and the belief in communication with the dead can be proved or disproved if earnest, well trained, emotionally stable people will tackle it as they would any other problem. It is my opinion that unprejudiced Christian ministers, more interested in teaching the truth of cosmic reality than in passing on previously formulated inherited doctrines, would make the best investigators in this field of study, especially if a few of them with scientific as well as theological training would dedicate themselves to the task.

"We need," he went on to say, "a scientifically controlled program of Christian psychic research within the framework of our established churches. People no longer are willing to accept traditional beliefs about immortality, by faith alone. Truth is truth, whether it resides within the realm of religion or in the field of natural law. All truth can be proven. Falsehood, whether it bears the religious label or not, cannot endure the test of scientific analysis. Falsehood, in fact, tends to shrink away from possible analytical approaches."

"But isn't this a forbidden area, according to the writers of the scripture?" I asked. "Can things of the spirit be seized from the universe and analyzed in a laboratory? Wouldn't it be an act of evil, tantamount to the building of the Towers of Babel, to subject God's Mind and Will to the scrutiny of materialistic scientific analysis?"

The stranger smiled and went on to say, "The innovator is always persecuted and is sometimes crucified. The human race is satisfied with the commonly accepted theories and opinions it has inherited from its fathers; it doesn't want these bulwarks of its emotional security disturbed. It always lashes out against the disturber. Anyone who attempts to introduce psychical research into the orthodox religious system will find that a tremendous wave of emotion, disguised as righteous indignation, will be hurled in his direction. But teachers of Truth must be prepared to accept such calculated risks."

I wasn't prepared to accept the man's entire statement as being true, but I did agree with his remarks concerning the fate of the innovator. Semmelweis had been ridiculed and persecuted when he dared to suggest that the doctors and medical students were responsible for the spread of childbed fever because they did not wash their hands before they went from their work in the autopsy room to attend the birth of a baby. George Stephenson's steam engine was looked upon as the work of the devil. Robert Fulton's steamboat was popularly named "Fulton's Folly."

As my newly acquired friend prepared to leave the train at Portland he cast this parting shot at me, "Think it over, Reverend. Someday you may decide to investigate my proposition. If you do, don't let the reactionary religionists or the orthodox scientists stand in your way.

"I believe that Christian psychic research and the science of parapsychology will supplant allegiance to credulous ancient dogmas, even as the science of non-materialistic physics is replacing the art of alchemy and its materialistic successor, chemistry. I think that honest investigators will find that life after death does exist and that communication can be established with that other dimension of life.

"I am a research scientist and not a theologian. My wife claims to be psychic and I am willing to accept her claim as a working theory which I can test."

He waved goodbye and disappeared into the disembarking crowd.

I didn't like what he had said. I had been trained as a chemist and was, at the time, finishing my education as a theologian. I had received training in both fields and felt qualified to speak with some authority on the matter. I decided to preach in no uncertain terms on the subject the very next Sunday and mail a copy of the sermon to the address on the business card this man had given me.

The next morning I stormed into my study. The result of several hours work was a stillborn sermon which I consigned to the wastebasket.

In the hour of meditation following my attempt I decided that my scientist friend was right! The church did stand in need of a Christian psychical research program to validate the claim of immortality it has made, without the offer of rational proof, down through the centuries.

I began to read in the field of scientific psychic research, parapsychology and the history of religions. I started to record the alleged psychic experiences of my parishioners and local townspeople, as well as the mystical claims of those who lived within traveling distance of my parish and seminary at Cambridge.

When people became aware that I was interested in psychic phenomena, they began to tell me their stories. I became something of a psychic detective, tracing stories of the supernatural back to their sources, in many cases visiting the alleged haunted houses and barns.

As a result I uncovered a great deal of fraud, deception, mental illness and wishful thinking. I also stumbled upon case after case of absolutely thrilling material which seems to indicate that there is something in this matter of personal human survival after death.

I came across enough evidence of alleged spirit communication to make me believe that here is a field needing intensive scientific and religious examination.

All over the world the Church of Christ is renewing its interest in the doctrines of spiritual resurrection and the Communion of Saints. It is no longer satisfied with vaguely affirming its belief in the "life everlasting" without defining what it means by this term.

The hour is coming when men shall not worship God on the mountain of theological abstraction or in the Jerusalem of outworn theology. Christ prophesied that the Father shall be worshiped in spirit and truth. Both of these can be verified.

The Spiritualists have broken the path in the quest for the Holy Grail of Eternal Life. Like the early Christians they have been persecuted and vilified. The charlatans and psychotics who have crept into the work of the Spiritualist movement have not helped it, but these people slink into the strongly defended fortresses of science and religion also. The movement is not to be condemned because of those who have misused its teachings, even as Christianity cannot be judged by those who profess it but fail to live up to its tenets.

Spiritualism, however, has only broken the path. Much work remains to be done by those, within and without Christendom, who can examine this problem in the light of an intellectual and scientific approach that is oriented to the philosophy propounded by Jesus on the shores of the Sea of Galilee. The established churches can do much to help explore, with the Spiritualists, that which is the common core of our respective faiths.

The traditional orthodox church and its ordained ministry has much for which to atone, insofar as its general treatment of researchers is concerned. It has allowed outworn theologies and creeds to deter it in its search for truth.

The institutionalized church had better not lag too far behind the parapsychologists and the psychical researchers. Such a lag could lead to its peaceful death. A new wineskin may be created to hold the eternal vintage of spiritual life. Just as Christianity, the spiritual Israel, replaced the ancient religion of the Hebrews, some other world religion with a new covenant may be the harbinger of the New Age.

Reverend Robert Elwood Allen: Minister at various Methodist churches in Maine; studied at the Harvard Divinity School, the Bangor, Maine, Theological Seminary, Simpson Bible College, Seattle, and St. John's Bible Institute, New York, among other institutions.

FATE September 1959

WHAT IT IS LIKE TO DIE
Jerry Stanley

On December 6, 1982, my heart stopped beating for 45 seconds and I was shown that there is life after death. I say *shown* because only that word conveys exactly what it was like to die.

I experienced no Great Truths. I did not meet dead departed relatives or my dead dog, Joe, nor did my life flash before me. I did not meet God. I wish I had; that would have been a Great Truth.

Instead, I experienced physical death and life after death. The first is difficult to describe, the second is nearly impossible to explain. This is why I haven't tried until now. It has taken me a long time to sort out exactly what happened to me and to select the right words to convey the experience. Here is the most accurate account I can give of my death which was, believe me, the ultimate trip.

Prior to the morning of December 6, 1982, I was noncommittal on the subject of an afterlife. At 41 I had good health, a good heart (I thought), a PhD in history, a secure teaching job with the rank of full professor and a loose connection to the Methodist Church. When the subject of afterlife crossed my mind, I just didn't know.

It was Monday, and other than turning in grades for the fall quarter, I had no plans. I was in the bathroom having my customary constitutional when the first pain hit. Within 15 minutes it had become wicked beyond belief and my left arm had gone numb. My terrified wife phoned the paramedics against my wishes!

Fifteen minutes later, when the ambulance crew rushed a gurney into my living room, I knew I was close to death. The pain grew until it felt as if a huge spear had been stuck into the middle of my chest. I was sitting on the couch dripping cold sweat and gasping for breath. When the paramedics laid me on the gurney I felt myself *going*.

Let me repeat: I felt myself *going*. I knew I was dying.

First, there was the physical sensation of being overcome. As I lay down on the gurney the pain spread from my heart to every part of my body, flaring outwards like ripples in a pool after a stone breaks the surface. At the same time, while the pain spread outwards, it disappeared and a new sensation came – a feeling I was being covered by a blanket. But it was no ordinary blanket. The blanket was inside me and as it covered me it grew in size. I knew life was going out of my body; I could feel it. But I couldn't do a thing about it. Then, when I was "all covered up," I had a split-second awareness of every part of my body all at once. It was like the flash of a bulb on a camera. Pooff! It was then that I knew I had died physically. I didn't think it. I didn't imagine it. I knew it. I was dead.

The experience of life after death started when the pain went pooff and disappeared. What I felt, at that instant, was a sudden awareness of self, an awareness of every part of my body all at once.

Imagine yourself underwater in a swimming pool. Recall how it feels to be completely enveloped by water and completely set off from everything. Now, subtract the water. In having an awareness of self, nothing else is experienced except self. I felt enclosed and set off, but I didn't know what I was enclosed by or what I was set off from.

Above all, awareness of self, at the moment of death, is nonphysical, unlike the feeling of being overcome physically. One is knowing. The other is feeling. Physical death happens gradually. Awareness of self happens instantly. Pooff!

The fact that I had just spent 41 years as Jerry Stanley did not present itself or matter. I had no knowledge of my accumulated self, my name, my experiences and so on.

Obviously, death was a state I avoided, that is, death as we normally think of permanent death. But I died. Again. I didn't think of myself as dead. I knew, through *awareness of self* that I was dead. And what occurred, after the moment of death, makes sense only as a death experience.

Our conventional idea about death needs to be revised. We tend to believe we are either alive or dead, one or the other. I think this is false. In all likelihood death is a process, as life is a process; it comes in stages.

After I experienced awareness of self, I experienced a process with stages or "stations." But before I experienced these stations I experienced three other things all at once.

I experienced light. It wasn't of any color, hue or intensity. And I can't say where it was because "everywhere" isn't a big enough word. To be as accurate as I can, I was in and of light of the kind that can't be defined as the opposite of darkness. It wasn't light, of course, but that's the only word we have for it.

I experienced a tunnel, knew of a tunnel. This will be confusing but let me say it anyway: 1 was in the tunnel and I knew what was outside it but I can't say what was outside it, only that I knew what was outside it! More important, I knew where the end of the tunnel was but not what was at the end of it. But here's the important point: knowing where the end of the tunnel was, was the most important thing about the tunnel experience.

Unable to experience anything except self, unable to see, I nevertheless saw the end of the tunnel. Here I don't mean I knew of the end of the tunnel. Here I mean I actually saw the end of the tunnel. I can't say how. I can't describe it. I can't say a single word about it. But I saw "it" and "it" was the only thing I saw when I was dead. It dominated everything associated with the tunnel. For example, I knew where the beginning of the tunnel was through the overpowering force of seeing the end of the tunnel.

As one of our most elastic pronouns, "it" can't be used to refer to the end of the tunnel. Nor can "the thing" or "the something." The only way I can describe what I saw, the end of the tunnel, is "the perfectly unknowable." Even the word "end" is misleading because direction, as we know it, doesn't exist in the passage to death. Direction only exists in that mysterious way by which a lost dog travels vast, uncharted distances to find his way home.

I knew no progression. By progression I mean a sense of purposeful, orderly movement. Again, I didn't "think" or "feel" I was moving. I knew I was moving – and not aimlessly. It was forceful, like the light and the end of the tunnel, which, remember, are all *one thing*. They all happened at once, simultaneously, and they are all *one thing*. I truly wish I could say what I was moving toward. If I said I was moving toward the end of the tunnel, it would only be a guess, maybe a good guess but a guess nevertheless. Like the end of the tunnel, my direction remained a mystery.

After I experienced the light, the tunnel and purposeful movement all at once, I started on my passage to death. Here I mean *one thing* ended and another began. The light, the end of the tunnel, the progression, this *one thing* that happened all at once became something new, and here's how it was new: I immediately recognized this *one thing* as a thing that had always existed and as a thing that is. In other words, the past and the present became one. The *one thing*, the light, the tunnel, the progression, I recognized as always having been and is.

Imagine a stationary train in the country. And imagine train "stations" with pastures and trees and pleasant landscapes between. Imagine that they have always been there, as we think of the word always. Now try to believe that you've just realized that you know for a fact that you've always been and are the train, the stations and the bucolic scenery. You don't know this because you feel it or perceive it with any of your senses. But you know for a fact that you and this scene are *one thing*. That's how I recognized "the thing," the beginning of my passage to death when the train started to move and take me to various "stations."

It's time to explain why I keep italicizing the phrase *one thing*. First, it's impossible to overwork this phrase in recalling my death trip. It's one of the main ways the experience is remembered. So far, I've used *one thing* to refer to the light, the tunnel, the progression. Now, let me say *one thing* refers to everything else I'm about to describe, such as the "stations" in the train analogy. Everything I've singled out to describe is just *one thing*. If I'm sure of anything it's that there are no "parts" to my death experience. There's only *one thing* and that thing is "I" in the passage to death.

I emphasize the phrase *one thing* because that's what I was saying from the moment of awareness of self through the entire death trip.

The paramedics reported that I said nothing. But I can still hear myself saying, quite literally, *"one thing, one thing"* over and over and over. Right now, I can hear it from four years ago, as if a sound recording has been implanted in my brain! I can't explain this. But I know when I hear those words I'm referring to me in the passage to death and to everything that happened to me while I was dead. Those words mean I'm dead. Those words mean I'm being led to and being shown the stations in the passage to death. Those words mean the whole experience is just *one thing*.

I started to experience what I'm calling the "stations" in the passage to death. I was the train, the train stations, the trees and all action that ever was and is, the *one thing*. But, for our purposes, I was also a passenger who was being transported, led. Along the way I was shown and knew of five things.

The word "frightful" doesn't describe what I felt. If you can imagine experiencing all of the terror that has ever been experienced by everyone who has ever lived all at once, then you understand what I mean by terror and what the first station was like.

What was I afraid of? Dying.

If death is a process – and I think it is – then I feared that process, meaning the stations or stages I was experiencing. I had no knowledge of what had ended, my career as a historian, my marriage, my life. But I knew I was dead! And so, I feared the dying process, what had already happened and was happening. In this cockeyed way, I knew I was dead and I feared dying.

I experienced progression. Let me explain what appears to be repetition. The sense of orderly movement I experienced at the moment of death changed. I recognized my new sense of progression as something that had always been and is. In a way, this new progression is like déjà vu except in déjà vu you only think you've had the same experience before. At Station 2 you know you've always had the sense of purposeful movement that's now happening to you.

My new sense of movement toward something was positive. Here I mean that I did not experience movement toward something good or great or blissful, but movement toward something positive, nothing more.

Accompanying this new progression – toward some positive end – is an overwhelming sense of being led and being shown. l recognized that I was being led to and shown what I've labeled the stations in the passage to death, so far terror and progression toward a positive end. Frankly, it was comforting. That's a good word to use if it's understood that I was comforted by the sense of being led and shown and not by what I saw, the end of the tunnel. To illustrate, I was comforted by the fact that I was a passenger on the train and by the fact that I was headed to a place that didn't terrify me because I'd already been there and had always been there. Let's assume that I'm still on the train but in this instance the train is moving.

I experienced inevitability. By this I mean the sense of being incapable of being anything else in the past or in the present.

For a change, let's switch from railroads to apple seeds. I know I am an apple seed. If planted, I'll become an apple tree, not a fig tree or a plum tree, but inevitably an apple tree. As an apple seed I'm not merely aware of this inevitability – I'm experiencing it! I'm experiencing my being as an apple seed, my being as a blossoming tree with limbs and leaves and my being as all of the apple blossoms on the tree. And I'm experiencing all of this all at once. This is what I mean by being aware of the inevitability of what you are and always have been.

I experienced assurance. I've chosen this word carefully. I mean a sense of security and safety. This is what Station 4 is all about. Now the question is what was I assured of?

I know the answer to this question but it's hard to communicate. First, I wasn't assured of life everlasting or death everlasting. I wasn't assured of God or of the devil. Above all, I wasn't assured about anything that we know of in what we call life. To be as clear as I can, I was assured that I was safe in my passage to death.

When I knew that I was safe in my passage to death, I spoke for the second and last time while I was dead. I know I spoke because after the tape recorder in my head plays *"one thing, one thing,"* it plays "it's not so bad, it's not so bad" over and over and over. I said that when I was dead and I can still hear it now. I was referring to me in the passage to death, to being dead and to dying, to the *one thing*, which now had become not so bad.

I recognized design. Again, this will be confusing, but I was led to and shown, made aware of design, meaning the first four stations were part of a design that was just one thing.

Here's the best I can do to convey this sense of design. Imagine that our railroad picture is a collage. Hundreds of pieces of paper have been cut to size and pasted next to one another to form the stations, the scenery and the train, which is now parked in front of the last station in the mosaic. Gaps separate the little scraps of paper so that the picture is fragmented. Now imagine the sudden disappearance of these gaps; abracadabra, the gaps are gone! Imagine that you are this fragmented picture and always have been and abracadabra, the gaps are gone!

Had I been able to know the design and not merely know of it, I'd be reporting a Great Truth here. But my passage ended at Station 5 and I don't know what was next. Something was but I don't know, and I won't guess. However, I know that everything that ever was, is, and that all of it is just *one thing*. And I know that this *one thing* is "I" in the passage to death and that it's not so bad.

The experience is indelible; it never fades. To hear it as it happens, listen to the actual memories:

- I am dead, I am me, I have always been, I am, there is only *one thing,* all of this is just *one thing one thing one thing.*
- There is light, there is a tunnel, there is an end to the tunnel.
- I am moving somewhere.
- There is terror, something is moving me, I am being shown it is inevitable.
- My movement is inevitable, my movement is inevitable.
- It's not so bad, it's not so bad it's not so bad.
- There is a design, this is certain, it's not so bad.

It took the paramedics 45 seconds to pound on my chest and zap me with 200 volts of electricity twice to bring me back to life. I opened my eyes and within seconds asked, "My heart stopped, didn't it?" I knew the answer, but I was back in a world where there's confusion, uncertainty.

The fact that I was dead for only 45 seconds may explain why I was kicked off at Station 5 and why I've nothing else to report. But let me say this: the most important thing about being dead is that we have an ability to understand it. It's almost impossible to communicate the death experience if you come back but you can understand it when you're dead.

Take my word for it: what waits for us is bigger than any of us have imagined or can imagine. Take it from one who has been there.

FATE December 1986

HEAVEN AND HELL

VISIONS OF THE NEXT WORLD
Paula Giovetti

Reports of near-death experiences and deathbed visions have been collected by parapsychologists for years, even if sporadically. The well-known Italian psychical researcher Ernesto Bozzano (1862-1943) published a great number of them in the Italian publication *Luce e Ombra* in 1906, 1919 and 1930. Bozzano's research was followed in 1926 by the publication of *Death-Bed Visions* by Sir William Barrett, a founder of the Society for Psychical Research in England. Today such books as Raymond Moody's *Life After Life* (1975) and Karlis Osis and Erlendur Haraldsson's *At the Hour of Death* (1977) are widely read. These researchers worked in different cultures, yet the accounts they collected were very much alike.

Because of my own personal interest in the subject, I decided to conduct a similar search for cases in my native Italy. I wrote letters of inquiry to various publications asking readers to send me their experiences. Within a short period of time I began receiving letters from people from many different social and cultural backgrounds. Only a few of them were familiar with the books I just mentioned, which made these cases all the more impressive.

Some of my respondents said this was the first time they had spoken of their experiences. Before this they have been afraid that other people would laugh at them or simply not believe them.

I eventually collected about 100 cases. I personally met some of the witnesses, spoke with others by phone and corresponded with still others. Roughly two-thirds of my informants reported purely personal stories of coming back from death, while the remaining witnesses reported observations made by the deathbeds of friends or relatives.

In roughly 40 percent of my cases, the dying person purportedly saw a dead friend, relative or religious figure coming to guide him through death. In several other cases the figure told the percipient it wasn't time to die and sent him back to life. Twenty percent of the subjects reported out-of-body experiences when near death; 40 percent saw lights, heard strange sounds, observed landscapes or reported other unusual perceptions.

Although it is not easy to break my cases down into discrete classifications – since several elements crop up in the individual accounts – I divided the cases into the following categories:

(1) Cases in which the subject saw deceased friends or relatives shortly before death.

(2) Cases in which the percipient saw or experienced a border, which was impossible to cross, between this world and the otherworldly realm. Also placed in this category were instances in which the dying person was sent back to life.

(3) Reports of out-of-body experiences.

(4) Unusual but pleasant perceptions of beautiful landscapes and related otherworldly milieus.

(5) Psychic phenomena that broke out in the environment of the subject's death, i.e., raps, psychic lights or apparitions seen by people who knew the recently deceased person.

(6) Reports contributed by people who attempted suicide.

Let's examine each of these categories in turn.

Deathbed appearances

As I pointed out earlier, this was the largest group in my study. Usually the dying person saw a deceased friend or relative inviting him to follow into the otherworld. For example, this report was contributed by a 77-year-old housewife from Cavereno, a city near Trent:

> I'll tell you what happened at the deathbed of my mother in February 1929. I was 18 years old at the time and the 13th daughter of my parents. Only I had survived, for my 12 brothers and sisters died in their early years. My father, a vicar, some relatives and I were with Mother, who was soon to die. She was lucid. Suddenly her eyes looked at the door and she smiled.
>
> The vicar said, "This woman is having a vision."
>
> Mother's eyes moved about the room and then she said, "Children, this is not the infant school..." Then she was silent because she was paying attention to something. Then she said, "All my... to give me the hand." She seemed to be examining the hands of invisible children.
>
> As she looked at their little hands, she said, "I have not even sufficient fingers?" Then she turned to us, who were listening in astonishment, and said, "All my children have come to take me, and I have not even sufficient fingers..."
>
> They were 12!
>
> More than 50 years have gone by since that day, but I remember every detail as if it were yesterday.

A similar case was contributed to my survey by a 50-year-old shop owner from the town of La Spezia:

> My husband died in September 1978 after several months suffering from metastasized cancer. He was never given

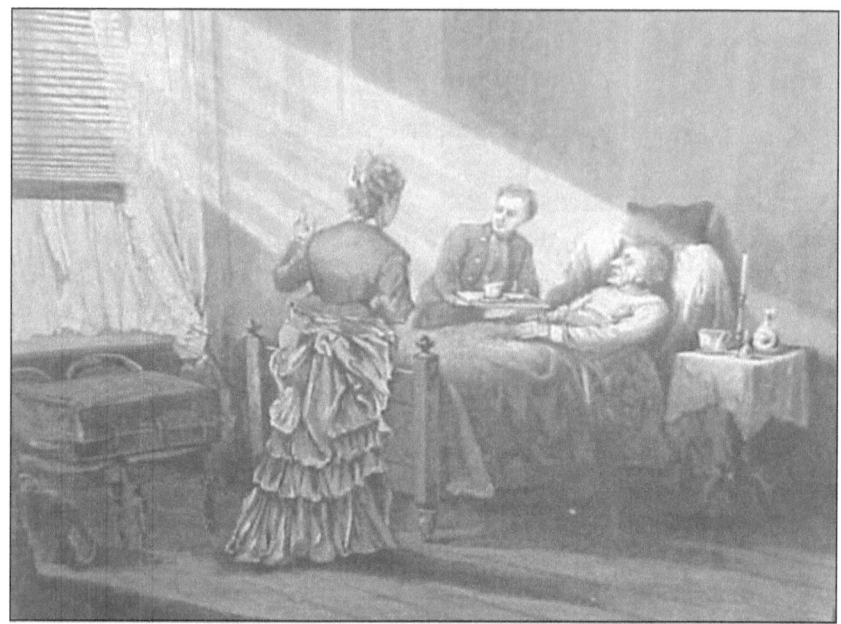

Author Hans Christian Anderson on his deathbed in 1875, bathed in heavenly light. Credit: Wikimedia Commons.

> sedatives. He was lucid and rational. On the last night [before he died] I was near him on a deck chair. He was then in a coma. I had fallen asleep. He called and told me in a feeble voice, "Adriana, darling, your mother [who had died three years previously] is helping me to come out of this awful body. There is so much light here. It is so peaceful." Then he died, leaving me this message of love, which helps me to live and to accept life without him.

Especially significant were those cases in which the dying person did not know from previous information that the deathbed visitor was, in fact, dead. For example, the case below was given to me by an elderly housewife from Leghorn:

> My nephew Luciano, a university graduate in conscription in Genoa, died in that town in a car accident. We didn't

have the heart to tell the truth to my mother, who was very old. We therefore let her believe that Luciano was engaged in a secret mission and would not write for a long time. She believed it.

When she was dying, she saw many dead persons in the other dimension and among them her grandson Luciano. "It is not true that he is alive; he is among the dead," she said. I was near her and I was astonished. She mentioned her father, too, whom she had never known during her life, because she was only two when he died.

Experiencing a border

Many dying persons experience a particular form of symbolism, for instance a doorway, barrier or wall, which keeps the patient from passing into the next world. Sometimes this is represented by a figure who declares it is not the patient's time to die. My first example is relatively short and was sent to me by a schoolteacher from Milan:

When my sister was 17 years old, she fainted and, falling down, hit her head against the corner of the marble table in our kitchen. When she recovered, she said that she had had a vision. She was in a large shining station full of people. Among the crowd our deceased grandfather came toward her, gave her a push and said, "Go! It is not time yet!" Then she came to herself.

Similar is a report I received from a 48-year-old journalist from a city near Trieste:

Last year I suffered from a high persistent fever and was hospitalized. Here my situation got worse and I entered a coma. My body was lying on the bed surrounded by doctors, nurses and my wife. I was above them and my mind was completely free. I had a sense of peace and happiness I had never experienced before. In front of me, in a great white cloud, I saw my father and my mother, smiling and waving to me to reach them. Behind them I saw other friends and old comrades-in-arms from the front where I once fought. In the middle of this cloud, a black-dressed figure – I'd say a vicar, with a shining face – appeared. I couldn't recognize him, but lifting up his hand, he got me to stop. Then all disappeared, and I came to myself in my bed.

A more conventional border was described by a nurse from Brescia:

Last October I was in a car accident and I was near death. It was a wonderful experience and I would never have gone back to earth and into my body. I was [floating] at the height of three meters and I could see everything from that position. I saw my car upside down, my dead body and the people assembling on the side of the road. I could hear everything they said. But then, looking up, I saw an enormous square of bright marble, as large as the world. At one end I saw a great wall and I realized that to go to the other world I had to cross that wall. I heard singing angels and I wanted to go and sing with them, but they refused, telling me that I had to return to earth. But I felt that everything is preserved there – I mean that thought goes on, even clearer [after death]. I was happy, blissful and shining.

Then I realized that I was getting smaller and smaller and I entered my body through my mouth and nostrils. When I came to myself, I was full of... wounds and pain. But my happiness was so deep that I did not feel my troubles. Only later, in the hospital, did I gradually begin to feel my enormous physical pain. The most important thing is that I was happy to see my dead body and I am no longer afraid of dying.

Out-of-body experiences

Two of the previous three persons described out-of-body experiences during which they encountered the barrier to the next world. As I have already noted, 20 percent of my cases included this effect. While experiencing particularly dangerous situations – such as being in a coma or car accident, during surgery and so on – the dying found themselves outside their bodies. They usually observed their physical bodies with a certain disinterest, feeling happy and peaceful during the episode.

A physician reported the following case:

> *I was with my family in S. Frutuoso (near Portofino, Italy) and I wanted to go and see a big statue of Christ which is submerged [offshore] at a depth of 10 meters. I am a good swimmer. When I was near the statue, I felt a sensation of immense peace and happiness and after a few moments I saw myself lying on the sea bottom, near the statue, breast and face against the sand. I saw the sunlight reflected on the sea and my [mental] state was of incredible and indescribable well-being. Only the desire to see my family convinced me to go back into my body. I went up like a cork, losing blood from both ears, and I was taken on board by a fisherman. When I was out of my body, everything seemed to me unimportant. Seeing one's own physical body is the same as seeing a dress you are fond of.*

A similar report, described in vivid detail, was contributed by a 26-year-old woman from Cologno:

> *Last year I had a terrible intestinal hemorrhage and I was hospitalized. During the night I was very weak and sad and without any energy. Suddenly I had the sensation of being above my bed. As a matter of fact, I could see not only my roommates but also a pale and starving body. It was my body, but it was as if it were not mine. I found it so insignificant and "not mine" that I thought, "How miserable I am! I look like a larva!" I was not afraid. I felt incredibly serene and happy.*
>
> *Then two shining beings appeared to me and said, "You must absolutely go back into your body!" I felt it absurd to be obliged to go back into that insignificant*

body, but suddenly I found myself inside it, feeling miserable, weak, full of pain and terror.

Like so many near-death survivors, this witness lost her fear of death through her experiences. Toward the close of her account she remarked:

Now I am pretty well, and I'd like to add that I am a young wife of 26 who loves life and cares for her body... I don't yet understand why that night I could be so unconcerned about it! One thing I wish to add is that, if at the moment of death, I feel the same sensation as I had that time, I won't be afraid to die. Death is not ugly. Only in the body do you feel pain and fear. I no longer have any fear of dying, but since that experience, I have loved life much more and I have tried to live it as well and fully as possible.

Landscapes and unusual sensations

Sometimes the dying person experiences a heavenly otherworld. Sensations of peace and harmony, similar to those reported in some of the previous accounts, are described.

A university professor from Catania reported such experiences when he suffered a coronary:

Last October I had a heart attack. I had just time to lie down. I clearly perceived the sensation of the end. I heard my wife weeping and I would have told her not to cry, because I felt I had reached a condition of ineffable peace and well-being, but I couldn't speak. For a while I had the impression of hovering in a huge, empty abyss with white walls. I found myself in peace and silence.

When I received medicine, my heart began to beat again, and I could hear and talk, but I cannot say I was satisfied with that. Now, after some months, I remember that absolute peace and silence – that imponderability in the white, empty abyss. Such recollections often return...

The professor ended his report by saying he often longs for the state he experienced when he was near death.

A bright, shining world was observed by a 60-year-old housewife from Genoa:

> Some years ago, I was in a serious car accident and I was brought to the hospital in a critical condition. I was in great danger and I was operated on. Before losing consciousness, I thought: "I do not want to die!" But suddenly I was lifted up by a multitude of angels and brought toward a light which became evermore bright. I was completely happy in that rosy atmosphere and I felt that the light I perceived was God, a good and infinitely loving God. I did not feel any desire or perturbation for what I had left, but only peace and sweetness for what I was waiting for. Suddenly I woke up and I felt that I was alive and that my son was holding my hand.
>
> After my son's death, nine months later, I often recalled my wonderful experience and it helped me in my pain. Today, I consider death as a reward and I am not at all afraid of it, because I know what it is: wonderful!

Psychic phenomena at death

In this category I include lights, raps, disembodied voices or crisis apparitions which seem to signify somebody's death. Generally, the phenomena are experienced by a friend or relative of the dying person. Less common, however, are those cases in which a stranger to the dying person reports the phenomena. For example, Dr. Christiaan Barnard, the famous heart surgeon, had just such an experience:

> I had this experience once as a patient in a hospital. While [I was] lying in bed in the ward, a woman entered, bent over me without saying a word, then vanished out of the window. Later I told a nurse about this experience and I described the woman. The nurse told me that a patient answering that description had just died in a room not far from mine at the time of my visitation. I had never seen the woman in life and did not know who was in the room

where she had lain. I cannot explain why she had come to visit me after dying.

An elderly housewife reported a related experience to me, even though the incident took place some 30 years earlier:

I am 65 years old and this is the first time I am reporting my experience. In the early morning of February 26, 1948, I was sleeping by myself; my husband had clandestinely embarked on a ship called the Valentina, *which had sailed toward Palestrina. I did not know that he had embarked. I believed he was in Italy, in Taranto, and I was greatly astonished when I heard his voice calling me, saying, "Leda, Leda!" I woke up, convinced he was at the door, but nobody was there, and I went on sleeping.*

Only a week later was the body of my husband found on the beach of Crotone. The Valentina *had been wrecked and my husband drowned in the early morning of February 26, 1948. But he had called me in such a clear and anguished voice that I woke up. After so many years, I can still hear that voice.*

Suicide

The following case reported by a potential suicide victim is the only such case in my collection. This case reads differently from the other reports in my files. The other witnesses spoke of feeling peaceful and serene, but not this witness:

Five years ago, I tried to die, and I remained in a coma for seven days. I woke up in a world of silence, convinced that I had done something harmful to myself. I had no physical pain. I felt light, restored and physically well. I was conscious of myself, my thoughts, sentiments and sensations. I was in a dark room. I was lying covered by a counterpane on a cold marble table. I was alone, desolately alone. I waited for something, anything, [since I didn't want to] remain in this state of mental anguish, which grew and grew.

I seemed to be in a spacious, austere chapel, which I felt was kind of a hospital. "My God," I thought, "am I alive or dead? If I am alive, I shall certainly die if no one helps me. A dead person would have flowers, someone there to weep..."

Suddenly I became aware of a dazzling light at my feet. It came from a beautiful gold lantern. Its white light shone directly on me. And in this light I saw a figure – young, pale with dark eyes, which fixed on me understandingly. I tried to communicate with him mentally. He answered in the same way.

"Help me," I called. "Help me, whoever you are."

"Be calm and have faith," he responded.

I became conscious of the sound of voices which grew louder. I mentally saw the upper floor: figures in dark clothes were talking about me. They were figures without faces, or perhaps their hoods hid their features. I was being tried, accused of having transgressed. I would have to pay. Though several figures defended me, a greater number accused me. I was terrified. Yet the being in the light gave me courage and made me understand that he could stop them if they condemned me.

Suddenly they burst into the room. There were many dark figures, old and bent. I felt their judgment was that they had condemned me. But when they tried to raise me, they could not advance. I escaped their hands because the light stopped them a few centimeters from me. They withdrew and I knew I was absolved.

The would-be suicide returned to life, but today she is still frightened of death. She is afraid that her "judgment" has been postponed and that she will have to pay when she dies. This case, so different from other near-death experiences in my collection, confirms what religions teach about suicide.

Anyone familiar with the publications and books I cited at the beginning of this article will see that my cases conform to those collected by other researchers, both in different countries and in different eras.

Although I have reported only a small selection of my cases, similar types of cases highlight my collection.

These reports were described in my book *Somebody Came Back,* published in Italy in 1981. It is, of course, impossible to prove the genuineness of these reports. We can only examine their common patterns, which recur time after time despite the great social, religious and cultural differences of the subjects I and my predecessors have interviewed. So, while such cases do not constitute formal proof, they certainly provide an indication that life exists beyond the grave.

FATE April 1989

SWEDENBORG: THE MAN WHO TALKED WITH ANGELS
Jerome Kearful

On a late Saturday afternoon in July 1759, a fire broke out in one of the residential sections of Stockholm, Sweden. Starting at six o'clock in a house in a district called the Södermalm, it spread rapidly and, before it could be extinguished two hours later, had destroyed a number of homes and considerable personal property.

On the same afternoon, an entertainment for a party of 15 persons was being held at the home of an English resident of the town of Göteborg, 280 miles distant from Stockholm. Among the guests at the home of the Englishman was the famous Emanuel Swedenborg. Swedenborg, a Swedish noble of an equestrian order, had returned to his native land from England only a few hours before and had been absent from his home in Stockholm for some time.

On the afternoon of the fire, the party in Göteborg assembled at about four o'clock. At six o'clock Swedenborg asked to be excused and went outside. He returned shortly, in a state of considerable excitement. A fire, he said, had broken out in Stockholm and was rapidly spreading in the direction of his own home in that city. The assembled guests received this information with mingled awe and incredulity. Some of them held property of their own in the same vicinity and could not disguise their apprehension as the Swedish scientist recounted the progress of the conflagration raging nearly 300 miles distant.

At seven-thirty Swedenborg reported that the fire was being brought under control. At about eight o'clock, he exclaimed: "Thank God! The fire is extinguished the third door from my house!"

This remarkable series of pronouncements by Swedenborg was soon spread about town by the other 14 guests and, on Sunday morning, the author of the strange recital was summoned by the Royal Governor in Göteborg. The Governor asked for, and received, from Swedenborg a minute account of the progress of the fire. Swedenborg gave him precise details as to how the fire started, the particular houses that had been burned, and how the conflagration had finally been extinguished. The Governor's interest in the matter excited the entire population, who thereupon waited impatiently for the next messengers from Stockholm. They arrived on Monday night and Tuesday morning – one from the Stockholm Board of Trade and one from the Royal Court of Sweden. Both messengers brought information about the Stockholm fire. It agreed in all details with the account that Swedenborg had related to his fellow guests on the preceding Saturday afternoon.

This strange and remarkable affair aroused the interest of Immanuel Kant, the giant of philosophy. Kant assembled corroborative information from distinguished and reliable persons in both Göteborg and Stockholm. He then published a summary of his findings with the statement that they placed "Swedenborg's extraordinary gifts beyond all possibility of doubt."

Kant's publication on the matter of the Stockholm fire appeared within a few years of the affair and within the lifetime of those who were concerned at firsthand. There was ample opportunity for denial or contradiction by the members of the Saturday afternoon party, the Royal Governor, or others who were personally acquainted with the facts and no denial or contradiction was ever made.

Startling as this and other similar feats demonstrating extrasensory perception may be, they were a mere incident in the

Emanuel Swedenborg.

remarkable life and activities of Emanuel Swedenborg, scientist, engineer, economist, theologian, metaphysician and intermediary extraordinary, between this and other worlds. For in Swedenborg were combined all these accomplishments, any one of which would alone have sufficed to monopolize the abilities and attention of most men. But this Swedish genius was no average man. At the age of six he astonished his elders with his mature talk about the principles of religious faith – and at the age of 84 he wrote a note in Latin to John Wesley in which he accurately foretold the day of his death a month later!

Between these two widely separated dates Swedenborg thought, experienced, acted and wrote with the most amazing versatility, originality and effectiveness. The range of his investigations traversed such diverse questions as the construction of canals and locks, the ethics of sex and marriage, the Swedish currency, the nature of heaven and hell and man's life therein after death.

He was the outstanding scientific figure of his day. He first formulated the theories of the nebulae and the galactic universes; he originated the science of crystallography and revolutionized the principles of metallurgy; in physiology, his discoveries suggested possibilities concerning the functioning of the human body that have not been fully explored to the present day. He left scarcely a field of science untouched – he excelled in geology, chemistry, mathematics. Nearly all his scientific theory was well over the heads of his contemporaries. No longer ago than in 1938 it took an entire bevy of modern specialists to report authoritatively on Swedenborg's scientific work.

Swedenborg's life, at least to the outward view, falls into two distinct parts. The first, during which time he completed his university training at the University of Upsala, traveled extensively in Europe and lived much in England, published the several volumes of his scientific works and served as Assessor to the Royal Swedish Board of Mines, ended in 1743, when he was 55. The second, during which he devoted himself solely to his investigations in the other worlds and to propounding his doctrines in connection therewith, covered the 29 years from 1743 until his death in 1772. Remarkable as was the first of these two periods in Emanuel Swedenborg's life, it is to the second and more startling span of his years that attention is here drawn.

Although Swedenborg's entry into his new mode of existence was symbolized by his resignation from his post of Assessor to the Board of Mines in order to be unencumbered in his activities, the roots and signs of the later man reach back into his earlier years – even into his childhood. Important, inasmuch as it persisted and was intensified in the later years, was the interruption of the usual manner of breathing, evident as a natural occurrence in Swedenborg while still a boy and youth.

Swedenborg considered this matter of the suspension of breath as of great importance in relation to his ability to visit the other realms and converse with spirits and angels. This phenomenon was only occasional in early life, when engaged in concentrated study or religious devotions. But later he studied the effects of rhythmic shallow breathing, breathing through the mouth, and suspending the breath entirely. With no physical respiration, he was able to "breathe inwardly" for an hour. He was not acting in ignorance of the functions of the human body, for no man of his time and few since have known more about physiology. Without control of breathing, he wrote, "the intense study of the truth is scarcely possible."

Another phase going back to Swedenborg's youth was his preoccupation with the question of the interaction of the soul and the body. The son of a Swedish churchman, he saw and heard so much doctrine and dogma preached that, as a young man, he determined to use scientific methods to investigate theological questions. While still a young man he combined experimental physiology with philosophy to form the basis for an inquiry into the body-soul relationship.

A third youthful sign of the later man was evidenced in his concern with his dreams. For a number of years, he faithfully kept a full diary of his dream life, recorded with scientific objectivity and impersonality. He added extensive speculations as to the physiological, emotional and religious significance of his dreams.

The vision, which he came to regard as a Divine visitation, by which the latter part of Swedenborg's life was ushered in, occurred while he was living in Amsterdam, Holland. Passing beyond the dream consciousness, he entered a state of "intense wakefulness," where, he says, he beheld the person of Christ the Lord. He "opened my sight to a view of the spiritual world and granted me the privilege of conversing with spirits and angels."

This was the beginning of Swedenborg's 29 years of alternately frequenting the "natural" and the "spiritual" worlds, almost at will. From that time on there was never any doubt in his mind as to the course he should follow. However, he was too much a man of the world not to realize the unfortunate reception that would be given any sudden pronouncement of the insight and powers that he had received. He took his new mission and calling as interpreter of the heavenly life and the servant of the Lord with the utmost seriousness and sincerity. He determined that his "truth by experience" could be fully and properly presented only in books, which might be read and pondered over by the thoughtful. He would write those books. And he did.

The books in which Swedenborg portrays the nature of the spiritual worlds and their inhabitants and propounds his moral and theological doctrines comprise some 20 titles and some twice as many volumes. Like his earlier scientific works, they were all written in Latin. They were printed in England at his own expense and, save for the writings of his last years, they were anonymous but for their description of the author as a "servant of the Lord."

In the Swedenborg cosmogony, the spiritual world consists of three principal realms: Heaven, Hell, and the World of Spirits. Each of these three is actually a world in itself, since only under exceptional circumstances is travel between one and another possible or permitted. Residence in the World of Spirits is, however, only temporary, since it is the clearinghouse for souls of the newly-deceased arrived from our natural earth world. After a longer or shorter stay therein, varying from a mere stopover to not more than 30 years of earth time, the individual soul finds its way into either Heaven or Hell, there to take up a permanent abode.

Everything in the spiritual world, in Hell as well as in Heaven, is subject to the Law of Love, an element of the Divine Being. After earthly death, the rule that like attracts like determines the eventual home of the spirit, whether it be among the glories and felicities of Heaven or the gross sensualities and evil circumstances of Hell. It often happens, says Swedenborg, that a man or woman who, on earth, lived a life of simulated worth and virtue, or another whom his fellows judged ignoble, go to the opposite abodes from what might have been expected. For one of the purposes of the World of Spirits is to see that all pretense, sham and hypocrisy is stripped from the soul. After that, the rule of like attracts like has full sway. Although Swedenborg explains that Hell is a necessary realm whose falsity forms an equilibrium with the truth of Heaven, his writings concerning that state are (as might well be expected!) comparatively brief beside his portrayal of Heaven.

Heaven itself is specifically divided into three worlds. These, in the descending order of their proximity to the central Deity, are called celestial, spiritual and natural heavens. The inhabitants of these realms are all angels of one degree or another. But, Swedenborg makes it plain, all the angels of Heaven have at some time been men who have lived an earth life. They always appeared to his sight in human form, surrounded by spheres of greater or less splendor and ethereality according to the state and station of the being.

Unique in Swedenborg's writings is the fact that he unfailingly put forward his teachings not as theological speculations or rhapsodical flights of the poetic imagination, but as actual records of observed fact. "Memorable relations," he called his accounts of his experiences in the other worlds. His books abound in such matterof-fact phrases as, "I have often talked with angels on this subject," "I have spoken with some who lived 17 centuries ago," or "I will illustrate this from experience."

If before the time that "his eyes were opened" he had been other than he was – an outstanding scientist whose clarity of thought and accuracy of observation were acknowledged by all, his subsequent words might have been dismissed more easily. But here he was, writing with the same spirit of observation and experiment about such fanciful things as angels, ethereal spheres, and the geography and constitution of the worlds of heaven!

He took a true scientist's interest in such questions as time and space in Heaven, speech and writing among the angels, and the various employments and activities in which the citizens of the spiritual worlds engage.

There are, he says, time and space in Heaven but they are not such as we know them in the natural world. The angels do not know these things as we do but only as changes in state. They know time only in relation to their own inward changes of love, intelligence and spiritual affections; they travel from place to place in the spiritual world according to the intensity of their interest and concentration on being in another place or discoursing with another. When an angel "goes from one place to another, whether in his own city or in the courts or gardens, or to others out of his own society, he arrives there sooner when he eagerly desires it and later when he does not; though the way is the same, it is lengthened or shortened according to the intensity of his desire. I have often seen this and wondered at it."

Angelic speech consists of sounds spoken by the lips and is used as a medium for the discussion of affairs much as on earth – "domestic affairs, civil affairs and matters of moral and spiritual life." The speech of Heaven is the same throughout all the realms and need not be studied laboriously for it is one of the perquisites of the angelic state. Its peculiarity consists in this, that the sound of the spoken word is a tonal replica of the thoughts or affections which the being wishes to express. Swedenborg notes the beauty and comprehensiveness of this speech and observes that the wiser angels, on hearing only a few words from a newcomer, immediately know and understand his state, his entire existence, and all of his past life.

It was to be expected that an author who had produced writings as extensive as Swedenborg's would be interested in writing in Heaven. Like Heavenly speech, Heavenly writing is a perquisite of the state. But, unlike speech, the forms of writing differ in the three Heaven worlds. The highest type consists of "curved and convoluted forms"; others are numerical, and still others similar to those forms known on earth. Whatever the form, angelic writing conveys to the reader in a few characters as much as a paragraph of earthly script.

The activities of the citizens of Heaven largely depend upon the particular "society" with which the individual is affiliated. These "societies" are "countless" in number. The number of individuals in each varies from a few hundred to myriads. A few of the special functions performed by the angelic societies as described by Swedenborg are concerned with: civil affairs and the general welfare; ecclesiastical affairs; the training of children (those who die as children on earth receive special instruction); protection of the unwary from attack by evil spirits; supervision of the souls in Hell; guiding those who are passing from the earth life to the World of Spirits or from that World to Heaven or Hell; and inspiring those still on earth to live a nobler life. Besides these and other activities, there are still so many more that they are "impossible to relate." Swedenborg does not overlook the fact that the angels also have their times of innocent entertainment and amusement. They even play tennis in Heaven!

From his astronomical studies Swedenborg well knew the vast extent of the material universe, reaching into the depths of remote space. He wanted to know the extent of Heaven. He says that he was shown that Heaven itself is boundless and will never be overpopulated. Moreover, he was told by the angels that there are many other globes populated by men similar to men of this earth all subject to the same Divine Law. He himself conversed occasionally with angels who had come from other planets, he says, and he wrote a treatise on that subject alone. Among other things, he notes that angels from Mercury, in accordance with their special state which is a love of knowledge of this kind, are "allowed to wander about and even to pass out of this solar system into other systems." This Swedish liaison officer between this and the other worlds emphasized two points as of the greatest importance: the nature of the Divine Being, and the Law of Correspondences. The one Supreme God, who created the entire material universe and the spiritual worlds out of himself is pure Love and Wisdom; on this earth, the Christ is his direct manifestation and the Bible his revealed Word. (A large part of Swedenborg's writings consists of explanations and interpretations of Biblical texts.)

By the Law of Correspondences, he meant that "the whole natural world corresponds to the spiritual world." Every phenomenon of man or nature exists and is caused by its direct spiritual "correspondence." Heaven as a whole, in fact, corresponds to the human form and each organ and member of the human body takes its characteristics from its spiritual counterparts in the Grand Man.

In all this complexity, and much more, Swedenborg found a unity. Heaven and Hell, the spiritual and the natural, truth and falsity, good and evil, all were bound up together to form the One. It was Harmony in Infinite Variety.

Swedenborg, of course, has been called hypocrite, liar and lunatic. His own homeland of Sweden for many years banned his books and fined and removed from public office officials who were discovered to be reading them. Even Immanuel Kant, who later produced eloquent testimony on his behalf, had earlier jested at his expense. A half century after the death of the Swedish genius, Samuel Taylor Coleridge named Swedenborg as one of history's "Great Men unjustly branded," and Emerson wrote at length in praise of him.

The attitude towards Swedenborg today varies considerably with the background and interests of those who come in contact with his works. While, in general, they look askance at "the self-deception and mystery-mongering" of his later years, scientists are giving a belated recognition to the importance of his scientific contributions. Psychoanalysts have concluded that he suffered from paranoia and an inverted Oedipus complex. Parapsychologists, more open-minded, have found his life a treasure trove for their investigations and speculations. Professedly occult writers avow that he contacted other intelligences on higher planes but that he misinterpreted much of what he learned. His religious followers, banded together in the contemporary New Church or Church of the New Jerusalem, hold that he was indeed the "agent of the Lord" and the harbinger of a New Dispensation.

The life of Swedenborg in his later years was one of remarkable equanimity. Numerous testimonies of those who knew him during that time agree that his manner was courteous, considerate and enlivened with moments of merry-making humor. He seems to have inspired affection even in those who were at first inclined to be hostile to him. He moved with equal ease in any rank of society.

The rulers of Sweden were his friends and supporters. Yet he found much that was agreeable in the company of humble tradesmen and artisans.

It was at one of his favorite London lodgings, with a wigmaker's family, that Emanuel Swedenborg died on March 29, 1773. A servant of the household reported that, "He was a good-natured man and a blessing to the house, for we had harmony and good business while he was with us."

FATE July 1952

IS THERE A HELL?
D. Scott Rogo

Is there a hell? Are some souls subject to eternal damnation after death?

Theologians have debated these questions for centuries. Certainly, many people throughout the world believe in an afterlife filled with unspeakable horrors, fire and brimstone being the least of them.

The idea of a place of damnation is not uniquely Christian either. The concept of "hell" was first formalized in the teachings of Zoroaster in Persia around the time of Christ, and early Christianity adopted the idea of hell and the devil from popular religious beliefs spawned by that prophet. Even certain schools of Buddhism, especially Amitabha Buddhism which is taught in Japan, teach the existence of hell. The Buddhist hell is so fiendish that by comparison its Christian counterpart sounds like a vacation resort!

But is there any scientific evidence for the existence of hell? According to one researcher studying the phenomenon of the "near-death encounter" (NDE), there is.

Dr. Maurice Rawlings is a clinical professor of medicine at the University of Tennessee at Chattanooga. Among his other positions, Dr. Rawlings is affiliated with the Chattanooga-based Heart Association's advanced Life Support Program and serves on the teaching faculty of the American Heart Association. His specialty is internal medicine and he is an authority on cardiopulmonary resuscitation.

This latter specialty has led Rawlings to the study of near-death encounters, which are out-of-body experiences many heart attack victims reportedly undergo during moments when they are near death or have actually experienced clinical death. The study of the NDE was first popularized by Raymond Moody in his 1975 bestseller, *Life After Life,* which described the experience as a blissful encounter during which the witness leaves his body, often travels down a tunnel to a heavenly paradise and there meets his deceased relatives before returning to his body. In the years since the book appeared, several physicians have replicated Moody's findings and have substantiated his research.

But Rawlings does not share Moody's rather idealized views about the afterlife. On the basis of his own research, he believes that hell literally exists and that some people who have had NDEs have actually previewed it! His book on the subject, *Beyond Death's Door,* has gone into eight hardcover printings since its release in 1978.

Rawlings's study began when one of his patients, a 48-year-old mail carrier, had a heart attack during a medical examination. The patient was undergoing a treadmill "stress" test as part of a clinical EKG when he went into cardiac arrest. Rawlings frantically tried to revive him.

"Each time he regained heartbeat and respiration," Rawlings writes, "the patient screamed 'I am in hell.' He was terrified and pleaded with me to help him. I was scared to death." As he continued working on the patient, Rawlings could see the look of abject terror on his face. Each time the doctor paused during the resuscitation attempt, the patient complained that he found himself slipping back into hell.

These visits to hell were not the end of the mailman's ordeal. Ultimately, he experienced a more peaceful NDE during which he "left his body," visited a paradisal world and saw his deceased mother and stepmother. The Tennessee doctor was in for a surprise, though, when he interviewed his patient several days after recovery. While retaining complete recall of his blissful out-of-body experience, the mailman had forgotten about his several close encounters with hell.

Is There A Hell?

This paradox has led Rawlings to suggest that many people on the verge of death may have a vision of hell but forget that fact because it is too shocking to recall. In his opinion this accounts for the apparent rarity of such reports. Nonetheless Rawlings went on to collect many other terrifying NDE accounts. He has published several of them in his book.

Interestingly, not everyone experiences hell the same way. These reports are less consistent than the more common Moody type of NDE. Some experiences seem modeled after the popular Christian conception of hell; other people appear to enter a Dantean inferno.

Thomas Welch, for example, has described an NDE he underwent. Rawlings quotes from Welch's 1976 book, *Oregon's Amazing Miracle,* with obvious relish. Welch had his NDE while working for a lumber company in Oregon. He was working on a trestle doing some logging work when suddenly he fell off and plunged into the river below.

"All I could remember is falling over the edge of the trestle," he reports. "The locomotive engineer watched me go all the way down into the water. The next thing I knew I was standing near a shoreline of a great ocean of fire. It happened to be what the Bible says it is in Revelation 21:8."

It was a lake of fire and brimstone, "the most awesome sight one could ever see this side of final judgment," Welch says. After the vision of the burning lake, Welch experienced a panoramic review of his entire life, after which a Christ-figure approached and conversed with him. Moments later he found himself back in his body, opening his eyes. He had been rescued by coworkers.

A very different nightmare NDE was reported to Rawlings by another of his heart attack victims. Although she didn't see a lake of fire, her experience was no less horrifying.

"I remember getting short of breath," she said, "and then I must have blacked out. Then I saw that I was getting out of my body. The next thing I remember was entering this gloomy room where I saw in one of the windows this huge giant with a grotesque face that was watching me. Running around the windowsill were little imps or elves who seemed to be with the giant.

"The giant beckoned me to come with him. I didn't want to go but I had to. Outside was darkness but I could hear people moaning all around me. I could feel things moving about my feet. As we moved on through this tunnel or cave, things were getting worse. I remember I was crying. Then for some reason the giant turned me loose. I felt I was being spared. I don't know why.

"Then I remember finding myself back in the hospital bed. The doctor asked me if I had been drinking or taking drugs. My description must have sounded like the OTs. I told him I didn't have either of these habits and that the story was true. It has changed my whole life."

Yet another of Rawlings' patients suffered clinical death while being treated for high blood pressure in a hospital. At one point during her treatment the patient lost consciousness and found herself traveling down a tunnel to a hideous cave. The rancid odor of decay enveloped the place and she saw half-human beings mocking one another. A Christ-like figure came to her aid soon afterwards. She then revived and was relieved to realize she was in her hospital bed.

"There are a lot of other things that may have happened that I don't remember," the patient said. "Maybe I'm afraid to remember."

Such accounts as these may not be as anomalous as Rawlings believes they are. Many people who have had spontaneous out-of-body experiences have reportedly wandered about in a misty, bleak world before returning to the body.

Dr. Robert Crookall, a retired British geologist and an authority on the out-of-body experience, has collected several hundred spontaneous cases. He discovered that while most people visit familiar earthly scenes during their astral travels, about three percent report a world not unlike the "hell" that some of Rawlings' informants describe. A few of his patients also speak of a world reminiscent of the realm of "tortured souls" that Emanuel Swedenborg (1688-1772), the great Swedish seer, described in his book, *Heaven and Hell*, which purports to be a report of his own visionary excursions into the realms of the afterlife.

Rawlings claims that victims of suicide attempts often have hellish NDEs. One 54-year-old housewife told the doctor that she had descended into hell after overdosing on Valium. After going through a black hole, she said, "I saw a glowing red-hot spot getting bigger and bigger until I was able to stand up." She was in a place that was "all red and hot and on fire... The earth was like slimy mud that sank over my feet, and it was hard to move." She prayed and awoke in a hospital room. She had been unconscious for two days.

But this unfortunate woman's experience isn't nearly so terrifying as one told to Rawlings by a medical colleague who helped resuscitate a 14-year-old schoolgirl who tried to kill herself with pills. After being rushed to the hospital the girl underwent cardiac arrest. During the only partially conscious moments of her initial recovery she related how demons had been grabbing at her during her brush with the afterlife.

Rawlings' research and case reports certainly are thought-provoking. Are the patients whose accounts he quotes really experiencing hell? Or can some other explanation be found to account for them?

These questions are difficult to answer. One problem is that few mainline researchers studying the NDE seem willing to deal with Rawlings' claims. I realized this in 1978 while attending a round-table discussion of the NDE at the 21st annual convention of the Parapsychological Association held at Washington University in St. Louis. Dr. Karlis Osis of the American Society for Psychical Research had organized the symposium and several leading authorities on the NDE presented papers at the meeting. Among these were Dr. Kenneth Ring of the University of Connecticut, Dr. Michael Sabom of Emory University, Atlanta, and Dr. Bruce Greyson, a psychiatrist from the University of Virginia.

Most of the participants reported that they had confirmed Moody's original findings. No one challenged the idea that the NDE is invariably a glimpse of paradise. No one mentioned Rawlings although his research had recently been published and many newspapers were discussing his findings.

After the session was over I asked Greyson about Rawlings' work. He said only that no one formally studying the NDE was coming up with the kind of data Rawlings claimed and that, in the view of some researchers, the Tennessee doctor was relying on improperly collected data. He did not explain what he meant by "improperly collected data."

Only one researcher has broken silence on the Rawlings matter since that time. Dr. Michael Sabom blasted Rawlings' book in a critique published in the November 1979 issue of *Anabiosis: The Journal of Near-Death Studies,* a publication of the Illinois-based Association for the Scientific Study of Near-Death Phenomena.

Sabom's attack was not so much against Rawlings' data as it was against the way the heart specialist collected and presented them. Sabom particularly criticized Rawlings' claim that hellish NDEs are rarely reported because most collectors of NDE cases are not actively involved in cardiopulmonary resuscitation work. Rawlings has long maintained that those actively engaged in this type of medical procedure do confront hellish NDEs.

But Sabom complained that Rawlings never has presented any statistics substantiating this allegation. He also chided Rawlings for relying on secondhand cases. Moreover, Rawlings' book does not explain how long after his patients were revived they told him their NDE stories. Sabom believes that after considerable time has passed revived patients may no longer have a very good recollection of what happened to them during their crises.

Sabom said that Rawlings' research is a "curious combination of medical facts, religious opinions, and poorly documented near-death experiences" and that his research "contributes little to the objective evaluation of the NDE."

Maybe – and maybe not. On one hand, Sabom's points are – academically speaking – well taken. Rawlings' level of reporting is not good, and he certainly does not adhere to the rules of proper data collection in compiling his reports.

On the other hand, Sabom's criticisms do not really address the central question. In fact, all his charges could be leveled as successfully against Moody's *Life After Life*. However Rawlings came by his data, the fact remains that negative or hellish NDEs have now been placed on record by obviously sincere informants. Sabom's review strikes me as an attempt to engage in academic nitpicking for the sole purpose of dismissing Rawlings' uncomfortable findings. But facts are facts, regardless of how one gets them. Any theory about the NDE must explain both classic ("Moody") types of NDE's and the types of cases Rawlings has been collecting.

It is possible these hellish experiences may be artifacts – hallucinations produced in reaction to the violent physical ordeals (such as chest poundings and electrical stimulation) which are part and parcel of normal resuscitation techniques.

Significantly perhaps, most of Moody's cases are taken from the accounts of heart attack patients, most of whom experienced close encounters with hell during the very moments of their resuscitation. The possibly hallucinatory nature of the experience may explain why, as Rawlings has continually pointed out, patients who have this kind of NDE may forget it after recovery. Most nightmare-like NDEs occurring as a result of suicide attempts seem to result from drug overdoses. And such overdoses might well produce hallucinations, colored by the percipients' own intense guilt.

Whatever the case may be, Bruce Greyson was not correct when he told me that no one engaged in the study of the NDE has uncovered data similar to Rawlings'. At least one researcher has.

Dr. Charles Garfield is one of this country's leading authorities on the psychology of death. He is currently a psychologist at the Cancer Research Institute of the University of California School of Medicine in San Francisco. Speaking before the 85th annual convention of the American Psychological Association (held in San Francisco in 1977), Garfield recounted his own research on the NDE. Of the 22 patients whose NDEs he had personally studied, he said, "four reported lucid visions of a demonic or nightmarish nature." Garfield was able to interview these patients shortly after their brushes with death. In striking contrast to Rawlings, Garfield found that "no significant changes in content were expressed by any of the patients in three interviews conducted at weekly intervals following the event."

Nonetheless Garfield's general conclusions echo Rawlings'. "It appears that not everyone dies a blissful, accepting death," he said. "Almost as many of the dying patients I interviewed reported negative visions [encounters with demonic figures and so forth] as reported blissful experiences, while some reported both."

So, is there scientific evidence pointing to the existence of hell?

Like so many questions dealing with either religion or psychical research, this one has no clear-cut answer. We can be certain, however, that the debate over the issue will outlive its current proponents and detractors. The researches of Rawlings and Garfield also indicate that the NDE is probably a far more complicated experience than investigators have believed.

Maybe Swedenborg was right when he wrote long ago that there is no single afterlife, that it consists of different levels, each with its own unique character. It wouldn't be hard to believe, if such is the case, that different witnesses may simply be contacting different realms of the hereafter.

D. Scott Rogo (1950-1990): Journalist, author and researcher on parapsychology topics; FATE columnist and frequent contributor of articles.

FATE December 1980

THE LESS THAN POSITIVE NEAR-DEATH EXPERIENCE

Barbara R. Rommer, MD

The term "near-death experience" usually brings to mind blissful accounts which include: the out-of-body experience; traversing a tunnel which ends in the bright, white, living, loving light; encountering relatives and friends who have gone before; encountering spiritual guides, angels or possibly The Being of Light; and often experiencing a full life review. Very little attention has been paid to the Less-Than-Positive (LTP) or frightening experiences, although my data suggests, thus far, that they occur with a frequency of 18 percent. They are, in fact, under-reported.

There are many reasons for this. Unfortunately, the LTP experiencers assume, with good reason, that their accounts will be met with harsh judgment. A large part of our society erroneously assumes that if a person has a frightening experience, he or she must have deserved it. There is also the probability that many researchers shy away from hearing about these distressful events. I absolutely disagree with the suggestion of researcher and cardiologist Maurice Rawlings, MD, that "negative" (I never use this term) near-death experiences are forgotten and buried by the subject unless they are questioned immediately upon being resuscitated after their (temporary) clinical death.

Actually, the opposite is true. Even when the person is interviewed half a century after the event, they remember it and describe it as though it happened five minutes ago. These LTP experiences are the catalysts for such phenomenal learning, self-introspection and soul growth, that the term "negative" is an absolute misnomer.

There is a Zen saying: "Now that my house has burned down, I have a better view of the sky." How true!

I define the Less-Than-Positive near-death experience as one which the experiencer interprets, in part or in whole, to be frightening, because it elicits feelings of terror, despair, guilt and/or overwhelming aloneness. Three types of Less-Than-Positive experiences were first described in "Distressing Near-Death Experiences" published in Volume 55 of *Psychiatry* in 1992 by Bruce Greyson, MD, and Nancy Evans Bush. Type I LTP experience is described just as a blissful one would be, but the subject perceives it as terrorizing. Type II LTP is usually reported as a black, eternal void, where the subject often feels bound. There are also often references to annoying sounds and shadowy or mechanistic presences. The Type III LTP contains truly graphic, hellish imagery. My research has suggested a Type IV LTP experience, where the life review specifically causes true terror. Here is an example of each type from my own research.

The Type I Less-Than-Positive near-death experience

"Nelly" was 67 years old when she developed severe chest pain at home and was taken by a 911 response team to the emergency room of a South Florida hospital. She had a cardiac and respiratory arrest (her heart stopped and she stopped breathing), and was clinically dead. She describes the event:

> *The doctors and nurses were running around doing things. My eyes were closed. My hearing was very acute but then, suddenly, I became stone deaf! Every sound stopped, but I*

could see! I moved out of my body into the room. I looked down on them and I saw my blue dress. I saw my body jump up when they shocked me. I was very, very scared because I couldn't hear them. Then I seemed to move into another area that was pitch black, like night time, like I was in outer space. I couldn't see a body on me. I couldn't see anything. I was petrified! I thought to myself: "I'm dying and I have so much that's undone: I didn't have a thing in order." I wasn't ready to go and knew I couldn't do a thing about it. And with that, just in a split second, I popped back into my body. I heard a man's voice say, "I got her." Then a woman's voice said: "We're not going to lose you again. You have to fight!" Then the cardiologist came, I had the angiogram (dye study of the blood vessels of the heart), and you know the rest.

I have found that most people who have Type I LTP experiences had never heard or read anything about near-death experiences prior to their event. They didn't know the light was coming! Most blissful NDEs begin with a moment of blackness. When one is resuscitated rapidly there is not time to progress into the light. Also, most Type I LTP subjects admit that they are used to being in total control of all situations at all times. This event is usually not under our absolute control.

The Type II Less-Than-Positive near-death experience

"Franz" was a well-known entertainer in New York, California and Rome. He feels that his spirituality reawakened in Rome, where he often went to the Vatican.

In 1971, at age 30, he returned to New York to perform in a nightclub. He left the club in the wee small hours of the morning with a lady friend. Despite the fact that he had been drinking large amounts of scotch, he drove the car. He admits that he was drunk. Speeding, he lost control of the car and hit a fence. His head hit the windshield and he was thrown out of the car, causing a concussion, punctured lung and multiple fractured ribs. The lady was instantly killed. Franz was out of his body, looking down on the scene, when he "heard" a policeman say: "I wouldn't give you 10 cents for his life."

He describes his experience:

Suddenly I was in a dark place going up very, very fast. I kept ascending. I had a great fear in that darkness. I knew I was coming from a bad place: drinks, drugs and the entertainment field. I had a short life review. I saw myself as a child and again in Rome. I cried out to Jesus: "I'm not in a state of grace, Jesus, let me live and I'll do it right." Then the dark, dark blackness became dark lavender and then I felt a sudden sublime serenity, a calmness like I've never felt before, not even in Rome. I felt He was there, and angels, too, a definite spiritual presence.

I guess I was shown the innocence of a child, and Rome, because I was so peaceful there and I had metaphysical experiences there. I guess I had to get in touch with that again because I was going back to my old ways. I was being shown that I had to shape up or ship out, one or the other. In other words, "get your act together": and I did just that. My life changed like night and day... I changed my career... I don't fear death... because I know that if I ask, I can live again. I know there's a life after life. I know there is reincarnation.

Of my Less-Than-Positive experiencers, 27.7 percent had this Type II variety. It is very significant that 54.5 percent of them had self-induced their (temporary) death, either intentionally or unintentionally through self-destructive behavior. Without exception, each and every one of them stated that the experience needed to happen in order to encourage them to make necessary changes. As Nietzsche said: "That which doesn't kill us makes us stronger."

The Type III Less-Than-Positive near-death experience

"Tyson," 21 years old, was "out drinking all night." He arrived home safely and went to sleep but was awakened "with a weird feeling and a headache." He became confused, reportedly had a convulsion, and was transported to the hospital.

He stated:

In the hospital I started to pass out and then it was dark. Physicians were shoving tubes down my throat and my nose. That was it. Then I was out, and they called a code blue. I'm just telling you what I was told. I was on life support by the time my family got there.

Then it went from reality to supernatural. It was extremely bizarre. I've only told my wife and you. Anyone else would probably think I was nuts. I was living a lifestyle that was very wild. I was doing a lot of things I shouldn't have been doing. I was basically a kid. I was going down the wrong path, hurting people, hurting myself.

Anyway, there was this supernatural figure. It was like a devil to me. He was very scary. He was the devil! He was a demon! I had no idea I was in the hospital. All I knew was that I was chained to a bed and I was being tortured. I could lift my head far enough to see this big steel double door with a small gap underneath. I could see and feel heat and flames. It was so damned hot that I felt like I was lying on hot coals. I'll be honest with you. I thought I was in hell. It was the most horrible thing you could imagine going through.

Have you ever come up on a possum at night, driving, and your headlights hit his eyes and they glow like beams? Well, that's what that demon's eyes looked like. His hair was extremely dark. He was wearing black, had really long fingernails, and he was extremely sweaty and agitated. And there was an even stronger force that was there, but I couldn't see a face, but it was talking to me. It was torturing me, too. It kept telling me: "You're going to die." And it would say other vulgar things. And I sensed monsters, hideous, horrible, and I could see their shadows and movements but not any faces.

I was raised Pentecostal. I was in what I grew up to expect hell to be like. I definitely felt judgment. I definitely felt I was there because I put myself there. I knew

I was going to be chained right there to that bed forever. Nothing was ever going to change. I do believe that if I had passed away then, for good, that I might have really been there forever.

This lifetime is a series of choices. Every second involves a choice. Nearly every near-death experiencer whom I have interviewed (now well over 400 of them) comes to know that each one of us must take full responsibility for these choices. As Aristotle said: "Wherever I go, there I am." Although we cannot escape our previous actions, we can certainly change our present and future behavior.

The Type IV Less-Than-Positive near-death experience

Aristotle also said: "The unexamined life is not worth living." When a life review takes the form of a tribunal, the experiencer may feel not only fear but also judgment from without. Ana Jo described her experience:

I found myself in a lovely wooded area with a pathway which I walked along. Suddenly, suspended from a sky was a stairway. I stepped onto the stairway and kind of floated up to a room that was also suspended in the sky. It had walls. The door was just an open doorway. It seemed to be marble construction of a cream and beige color. Along either side were tables set up. There were individuals behind, seated along the tables all the way down, but I could not discern their faces. They were in spirit.

I walked to the far end, and there was a table like this one, where three people sat. And I found myself on trial before a tribunal, for either something I hadn't done or something I had done. I don't know what it was. I wept. I knew I was in trouble. Then the person in the middle of the three said: "Go, you have your instructions." I turned around and was walking out. A master teacher stepped out from one of the tables. I know I remembered him from somewhere. He was a spiritual teacher. He walked out with me to the doorway. As I was coming down the stairway I knew I'd been given a second chance to correct whatever I'd done wrong.

Reasons why a Less-Than-Positive experience occurs

I believe that there are three primary reasons why a Less-Than-Positive near-death experience may occur, rather than a blissful one. First and foremost, it may occur to challenge one to stop, look back and re-evaluate all previous choices, actions, reactions, thoughts and words in order to make beneficial midcourse changes in direction. Second, it may occur if the experiencer has a Less-Than-Positive, or less-than-loving or fearful mindset immediately prior to the event. Third, if one grows up with negative programming expecting hell, fire and brimstone, then that is what he or she projects to the cosmos and that is what may be experienced.

I view the Less-Than-Positive near-death experience as the ultimate learning experience. Obviously, it can take time to integrate this type of event into one's life, especially if one doesn't talk about it or get help in dealing with it. There are many support groups of the International Association for Near-Death Studies around the world. We invite all near-death experiencers to join us in a very safe, loving, spiritual and supportive environment to discuss these events. My book, *Blessing in Disguise: Another Side of the Near-Death Experience* discusses both the Less-Than-Positive and the joyful near-death experiences.

Dr. Barbara Rammer: Physician with an internal medicine practice; a member of the Board of Directors of the International Association for Near-Death Studies.

FATE August 2000

JUDGMENT DAY!
Michael Newton

In my practice as a hypnotherapist I have worked with genuinely good people who feel they are inherently bad. Regardless of how much they give of themselves to others, it is never enough. These individuals think evil exists within them and they are going to pay dearly for all their transgressions at the moment of death. I often find much of this negativity is the result of mental conditioning they received as children – particularly in rigid, fundamentalist households. It is the belief of these people that, eventually, they are going to be taken into an underworld of torment and harshly judged, no matter what they do in life.

Within the structure of the world's major religions there are theological elements of great beauty but also dictums of ugliness. Frequently, one finds segments of strict fundamentalism that gravitate to the ugly side with long-standing beliefs in a satanic kingdom waiting to punish wrongdoers after death. In my opinion, these dire predictions of "ultimate truth" were originally founded to establish fear as a means of controlling people. To intimidate impressionable people by scaring them about a hell in the hereafter is cruel. This form of persecution and brainwashing fosters the dread of death which begins in childhood and grows with age. Crossing into the afterlife is something to be feared.

In the six years between the publication of my first book, *Journey of Souls* (1994), documenting case studies of life between lives, and my book, *Destiny of Souls* (2000), I have been traveling around the country talking to audiences about the ordinary people who make up my cases. Since spiritual regression is my area of hypnosis specialization, these clients come in order to mentally be taken back to the time of their soul existence between former lives. I wrote *Destiny of Souls* to provide further detail about what I have learned of the spirit world in response to the many questions I received about life after death on these lecture tours. At the top of the list of public inquiries were concepts of judgment and punishment in our afterlife.

When I explain at lectures that, in all my years of research, no case of mine has seen or experienced any sort of hell after death, someone invariably raises their hand to ask about the less than positive NDE (near-death experience) cases reported by the press. People want to know how I reconcile my case reports of light, peace and love with the sensationalized stories from certain NDEs who say they did not see bright lights but experienced only cold darkness and an atmosphere of hell. There is an account from one NDE who said he was hauled before a tribunal of judges by screaming ghouls to answer for his sins before being "rescued" by returning back to life.

There are a number of responsible writers of the less than positive NDE who consider these occurrences as a self-inflicted wake-up call by people to make better use of the time they have left after returning to life. This does not mean we are going to be punished for disbelieving in God or avoiding participation with institutional religion. My own view is that the few NDEs who report they have seen hell were stuck in the tunnel between life and death for a few brief minutes and never entered the light because their time in a death state was so short. Their experience was so brief they did not even see spiritual guides. Consider too, that the negative frame of mind they might have had just prior to this bad experience and the fact that the coldness of their physical bodies and the noise around them (amplified to screaming) while unconscious are also contributing factors.

Gustav Doré's concept of the Last Judgement, 1866.

I feel there are highly susceptible individuals who were preconditioned by strict religious programming into believing in the existence of a hellish place before their negative NDE. They carried these mental images of horror with them during the actual physical trauma they suffered which involved a loss of consciousness. In the quiet, relaxing state of hypnosis, a physically healthy person describing a former death scene to me does not perceive heat, cold, loud sounds or frightful visions of a court of last resort waiting for them on the other side. We discuss how they entered the spirit world, who meets them, where they go and what they do as a soul.

After working with hundreds of cases over many years, I have found a remarkable consistency to their reports about the afterlife. Without devaluing the less than positive near-death experience, these individuals make up only a distinct minority. Most NDE people relate the same sort of images of the spiritual gateway as my clients in the early stages of hypnosis. What is seen on the other side is very empowering.

Is there any basis of reality for our mental images of being judged in the afterlife? I have the conviction that certain cultural myths are not simple, made-up stories with no practical foundation in soul memory. All my subjects tell me that after every life they do go before a panel of wise beings. Sometimes they call them judges, but more often I hear such terms as directors, masters and elders. These spiritual beings do not appear to be arbiters who pass sentences and exact punishment for misdeeds. The words "courtroom" and "trial" are never used by hypnosis subjects to describe these proceedings. In my view, the superconscious memories of these events between our lives come back to us in flashbacks and dreams. However, these images may be distorted by the conscious mind. In these instances, the spiritual event is equated and subverted by earthly concepts of demons, spiritual courts of law and retribution.

Based upon my client's statements, I have come to call our spiritual board of review the Council of Elders. Because of so many inquiries from people about a time of judgment, I devote a whole chapter in *Destiny of Souls* to this soul experience in the afterlife. The Elders on our councils vary in number and are typically seen wearing white robes. Frequently, our personal spiritual guides accompany us to these gatherings, not as defense attorneys but rather to assist in the interpretations. Unlike many Hollywood movie scripts which depict adversarial spiritual courts, we are not grilled unmercifully about our mistakes in life. The first question generally put to us is, "Well, do you think you achieved your goals in the last life?"

The following case quote from a subject in hypnosis is an illustration of a spiritual judgment scene: "The faces of the Elders in front of me are kindly and they are here to help me evaluate the life I just lived. My guide is with me. She provides support for me as we review my achievements and shortcomings in the last life. I am expected to express my frustrations in the past life and desire for the type of new life I wish in future. The Elders are honest and open with me and I am always treated fairly."

Many of my subjects see these wise beings as males and females while others consider them as gender neutral. The settings are always quiet, dignified and respectful to the soul. A council chamber environment contrasts with the busy social group activity of souls described in my books. Another example of a judgment scene taken from *Destiny of Souls* comes from a subject who, upon leaving the council, said: "When the elders are finished with me I feel they told me much more about what I did right than where I went wrong. The council knows I have had critical meetings with my guide about my performance. They don't patronize me, but I think part of their job is to raise my expectations. The council says they foresee great things from me. The last thing the Elders said was to stop looking to others for self-validation. When I leave them, I feel they have absorbed all my self-doubt and cleansed me."

I find in my travels around the country that many people are more fearful about what happens to them after death than about death itself. My message is that the spirit world is surrounded by forgiveness and high expectation for our growth potential. Certainly, those people who have been involved with evil acts will pay their karmic debts in future lives. However, they will not be sent into a place of eternal damnation and despair with no hope of redemption.

Michael Newton, PhD (1931-2016): Counselor, hypnotherapist and author; founder of The Newton Institute for Life Between Lives Hypnotherapy.

FATE August 2000

About FATE Magazine

Six decades before reality TV shows and late-night radio's *Coast to Coast AM*, and countless websites, blogs, books, and movies began captivating audiences with true tales of UFOs and the paranormal – there was FATE – a first-of-its-kind publication dedicated to in-depth coverage of mysterious and unexplained phenomena.

FATE was a true journalistic pioneer, covering issues like proof of survival, electronic voice phenomena, life on Mars, telepathic communication with animals, and UFOs at a time when discussing such things was neither hip nor trendy. Today FATE enjoys a rare longevity achieved by only a few similar US periodicals.

How it all began

The year was 1948. The Cold War was in its infancy, and the Space Age was still a dream… but across the nation and around the world, people observed strange objects flying through the skies.

Two Chicago-based magazine editors, Raymond A. Palmer and Curtis B. Fuller, took a close look at the public's fascination with flying saucers and saw the opportunity of a lifetime. With help from connections in the worlds of science fiction and alternative spirituality, they launched a new magazine dedicated to the objective exploration of the world's mysteries. They gave their "cosmic reporter" the name FATE.

FATE's first issue, published in Spring 1948, featured as its cover story the first-hand report of pilot Kenneth Arnold on his UFO sighting of the previous year, an event widely recognized by UFO historians as the birth of the modern UFO era.

FATE's ongoing coverage of survival after death

FATE has covered a wide range of topics during its lifetime. From the beginning, it has provided steady coverage of survival after death and related topics, such as near-death experiences, mediumship, dreams and communication with the dead. Every issue of FATE – more than 730 to date – has included personal testimonies of experiences that have convinced people that death is not the end.

Relevant today
In a fast-paced, high-tech world that is often short on attention span and long on cynicism, how does a magazine like FATE continue to thrive? Editor-in-Chief Phyllis Galde says, "FATE allows readers to think for themselves by providing them with stories that mainstream publications don't dare touch. The truth is, reality does not conform to the neat and tidy box that many people would like to wedge it into. Our world is a bizarre and wondrous place and our universe is filled with mystery – it is teeming with the unknown. People are longing for something more than the mundane transactions of everyday existence. FATE feeds the soul's appetite for the enigmatic, the esoteric, and the extraordinary."

Subscribe to FATE
FATE is published in intervals throughout the year in a popular digest size. Join the family of subscribers by visiting the FATE website at www.fatemag.com.

About Rosemary Ellen Guiley

Rosemary Ellen Guiley, executive editor of FATE magazine, is a leading expert in the metaphysical and paranormal fields, with more than 65 books published on a wide range of paranormal, UFO, cryptid, spiritual and mystical topics, including nine single-volume encyclopedias and reference works. Her work focuses on interdimensional entity contact experiences of all kinds (spirit, alien, creature), the afterlife and spirit communications, psychic skills, dreamwork for well-being, spiritual growth and development, angels, past and parallel lives, and investigation of unusual paranormal activity. She has worked full-time as an investigator, researcher, author, and presenter since 1983, and spends a great deal of time in the field doing original research.

Rosemary is president and owner of Visionary Living, Inc., a publishing and media company; its publishing division is Visionary Living Publishing, specializing in nonfiction and fiction books on paranormal and metaphysical topics. Visit www.visionarylivingpublishing.com.

A personal note from Rosemary

I have been privileged to be part of the FATE family since 1991-92. Dennis Stillings, the publisher of *Artifex* magazine, introduced me to Phyllis Galde and David Godwin, editors of FATE. They invited me to contribute to the magazine, and a lasting friendship was struck.

I started as a columnist, joining a prestigious company of other FATE columnists and regulars, among them John A. Keel, Mark Chorvinsky, Loyd Auerbach, Antonio Huneeus, and Loren Coleman.

In the early 2000s, Phyllis and David purchased FATE from Llewellyn Worldwide Publications. David passed in 2012, and FATE remains under Phyllis' ownership.

Over time, I went from columnist to consulting editor, and in 2016 became executive editor, taking on more editing responsibilities. Phyllis and I entered into a partnership to publish a series of books on the best from the archives of FATE on timeless topics of ongoing interest. FATE has thousands of excellent articles in its vaults, written by the best of the best, and I am pleased to make many of them available again.